SIMON &
SCHUSTER
EDITIONS

Other books by Marcel Desaulniers

THE TRELLIS COOKBOOK

DEATH BY CHOCOLATE

THE BURGER MEISTERS

DESSERTS TO DIE FOR

AN ALPHABET OF SWEETS

DEATH BY CHOCOLATE COOKIES

MARCEL DESAULNIERS

Salad Days

Main-Course Salads
for a First-Class Meal

SIMON &
SCHUSTER
EDITIONS

SIMON & SCHUSTER EDITIONS

Rockefeller Center

1230 Avenue of the Americas

New York, New York 10020

Designed by Karolina Harris

Manufactured in the United States of America

1   3   5   7   9   10   8   6   4   2

Library of Congress Cataloging-in-Publication Data

Desaulniers, Marcel.

Salad days: main-course salads for a first-class meal/Marcel Desaulniers.

p.   cm.

Includes bibliographical references and index.

1. Salads.   2. Entrées (Cookery)   I. Title.

TX740.D468   1998

641.8'3—dc21   97-47083

CIP

ISBN 0-684-82261-X

To my daughter Danielle

Let first the onion flourish there,
Rose among roots, the maiden-fair,
Wine-scented and poetic soul
Of the capacious salad bowl.
— ROBERT LOUIS STEVENSON

Acknowledgments

Salad Days, as with any book, was not a solitary endeavor. My sincere thanks go to: Connie Desaulniers, for the constant love and inspiration; Dan Green, for being a lion of a literary agent; Penny Seu, for her careful editing; Danielle Desaulniers-Shepherd, who supplied me with contemporary wine wisdom; Brett Bailey, who assisted me in completing the recipe testing for this book; Kelly Bailey, for her baking expertise and the motivational cookies; John Curtis: lucky for me to have such an outstanding business partner; Trellis chef Michael Holdsworth and senior assistant chef Steve Francisco, for their outstanding culinary support; Nancy Thomas and Audrey Julian: through their encouragement and expertise, the herb garden at Ganache Hill flourishes; Eileen Freidman, for the idea that launched lots of delicious salads; Janice Easton, Simon & Schuster, for the title and first-class editing; Melissa Golden, Simon & Schuster, publicist extraordinaire; William Rosen, Simon & Schuster, for making the decisions; all the kitchen, front-of-the-house, and office staff at The Trellis, for striving for excellence; my mother, Victoire Desaulniers, who would rather eat chocolate than salad; Clementine Darden and Gisele Hicks, for more than seventeen years of exemplary service preparing salads and much more in the Trellis pantry; The Culinary Institute of America, for the best culinary education then and now.

Salad Days

Contents

Greens

Beans

Grains

Fruits

Introduction

Don't let the name *Salad Days* fool you into thinking this book is about health food. No scrawny, naked greens clinging to a stark plate, begging for attention, are found here. No macrokilocaloric counts to confuse the cook into presenting fiber first, taste last. No fat grams quizzes, no new math sodium counts, no good-versus-bad cholesterol puzzles. Instead, *Salad Days* is about delicious and luxuriant food (*psst*—that happens to be healthy).

Like stepping from Dorothy's insular, gray, and crumpled abode into the great and colorful Oz, the recipes in *Salad Days* are lush and exciting. The only difference is that you'll never want to go "home" again to the two-dimensional, monochromatic salads of health food days gone by. And the choices are endless: vegetarian versions that are lavish on their own with texture and spice, or partnered with an indulgent source of protein; a multitude of dressings from lean to lascivious; greens so fragrant, colorful, and zesty that you'll understand why they call the other "iceberg."

We are fortunate to live in a time in which exotic products from faraway cultures are as close as the local market and when science has accommodated our year-round desires for the best and freshest produce. *Salad Days* will guide you to finding these products and show you how to use them and how to improvise when necessary.

Salads are no longer an afterthought but are truly the highlight of a meal—first-class main course salads.

Marcel Desaulniers
Ganache Hill
Williamsburg, Virginia

Salad Days at Ganache Hill

HIGH ON THE HILL

In the spring of 1996, I entered a new phase in my life—I moved to Ganache Hill. I don't actually live at Ganache Hill, but I develop, test, and write recipes for my cookbooks there, so I guess you could say my "culinary" heart is there. Located just four miles from my restaurant, The Trellis, Ganache Hill is a dream come true. Picture a small (1,600 square feet) bungalow, perched on a hilltop decked with mature white pine, dogwood, magnolia, crepe myrtle, pecan, and oak trees. An herb and flower garden welcomes you as you approach the entrance, tantalizing you with aromas that refuse to dissipate even after you close the front door.

Once inside Ganache Hill, you are struck by the contrast of the cozy cottage-inspired exterior and the open-air interior. Most of the second floor was removed to create a cathedral-ceilinged studio (for food and film photography), letting in a flood of light from a sun-shaped window above. The walls that are not lined with bookcases (holding more than one thousand cookbooks) display contemporary, folk, and outsider art with a food-related theme.

It is no surprise that the kitchen is the heart of Ganache Hill. By far the largest room, the kitchen is outfitted with top-of-the-line home appliances, not behemoth commercial ranges and ovens found in restaurants. This way I can create reliable recipes with the same appliances that are used by home consumers.

Personal computers make a presence, with a laptop in the kitchen and desktop systems in my first-floor office and my assistant's second-floor space.

Salad Days is the second cookbook (*Death by Chocolate Cookies* was the first) developed and tested at Ganache Hill. My previous books were tested in my home kitchen (which has a remarkable lack of space). Given the delightfully accommodating environment at Ganache Hill—and, it is hoped, your continued interest—many more books will follow.

THE SCALLION IN WINTER

Most recipes for *Salad Days* were tested from January through March 1997. It may surprise you that this is a matter of exultation rather than lamentation. How could one not rejoice when the availability of diverse foods is so bountiful no matter the time of year? Certainly we had no difficulty in finding rutabagas, parsnips, beets, fennel, Belgian endive, arugula, and spaghetti squash. But neither were we disappointed when we looked for bok choy, jicama, ginger, red raspberries, and papayas.

Although I have social and professional concerns about where foods are grown and when and how they are brought to market, I succumb to my passion for flavor in deciding what we serve at The Trellis. Likewise, the consumer should not be swayed by those scribes who would have us eating only what we can harvest from our backyard gardens. We should instead be thankful that science, airfreight, and the availability of fresh ingredients from the global farm enable the cook to procure and enjoy an extraordinary variety of foods year-round.

Allow me to emphasize that we purchased *all* the ingredients utilized to test the recipes in *Salad Days* at markets in Williamsburg, Virginia (the one exception is sea scallops), rather than using the nationwide network of purveyors that supply foods served at The Trellis. I'm not bragging about our markets in Williamsburg; I am encouraging you to be open-minded about the extraordinary availability of ingredients that can make every meal an exciting rather than an ordinary event.

TOO LITTLE OR TOO MUCH

On my first visit to the Canyon Ranch Spa in Tucson, Arizona, in January 1987, I had an epiphany of sorts. Confronted with a high cholesterol reading (285 mg/dl) and eschewing medication, I decided to embark on a totally vegetarian diet. It worked. In just six weeks of a strict vegan diet I experienced more than a 30 percent reduction in my blood cholesterol level. I was gratified that I could change a potentially health-threatening situation with diet. Unfortunately, as a long-distance runner, my vegetarian diet did not provide the correct levels of nutrients to maintain my desired weight and muscle mass. In fact, during a routine visit to my internist and friend of many years, Dr. William Massey, I was prescribed 4 ounces of red meat per week as a cure for my gaunt cheeks and concave chest. That, or learn how to balance a vegan diet suitable to my lifestyle.

Although I am no longer on a vegan diet, many of the meals I consume on a weekly basis are meatless. But because of my exercise regimen and my career as a chef, I choose to eat some form of animal protein several times a week. I find that consuming smaller portions (3 to 5 ounces) of meat, fish, or poultry, usually at my midday meal, allows me to maintain my correct weight without exponentially increasing my cholesterol level. Having said that, I confess to a healthy appetite; consequently, the portion sizes of the main course salads in *Salad Days* are substantial. I did eat every one of these salads to ensure that the average consumer would be sated by the portion size as suggested in the recipe. Although all the salad recipes in the book yield four servings, I am certain that some of them can be extended to make six and even eight without increasing the amount of ingredients in the recipe. If you do this and also serve one of the variations, you need only increase the number of portions of salmon, chicken, or whatever the variation may be to coincide with the number of salads you choose to have the recipes yield.

H O T   A N D   C O L D

Things change, and so do aphorisms. I remember being lectured during my early years in the culinary profession "that hot foods should be served hot and cold foods cold." Happily, this rule changed when some iconoclastic cook with a brilliant palate discovered that many foods benefit by being served at temperatures neither hot nor cold. This gets tricky for restaurants, since the Health Department frowns on foods being held in the temperature range of 40 to 140 degrees Fahrenheit (the so-called "danger zone"). This is a valid reason for concern because foods that are held for extended periods of time in this "danger zone" are ripe for the growth of bacteria. Although I would caution the consumer, I do not hesitate to recommend serving several of the salads in *Salad Days* at room temperature rather than straight from the refrigerator. Dishes such as White Bean Salad (see page 73), Pears and Caramelized Onions (see page 184), Marinated French Lentils (see page 85), and many more may safely be held and served at room temperature following the guidelines described in the recipes. Simply stated, they all taste substantially better when they are not refrigerator cold. Additionally, foods served at different temperatures surprise the palate and awaken the senses (need I remind you of a hot fudge sundae?). Take the salad (on page 135) of Arborio Rice Cakes (served hot) with Marinated Plum Tomatoes, Artichokes, and Sweet Peppers (served at room temperature) on a Bed of Leaf Spinach (served chilled) with Saffron Oil Vinaigrette (room temperature), and you have the perfect juxtaposition of textures and temperatures on each delicious forkful.

M I X   A N D   M A T C H

Necessity may be the mother of invention, but for me it is curiosity that squeezes my creative juices. I am always amazed when someone does not create a recipe because a certain ingredient is not available. "I was savoring the thought of your pheasant with fingerling potatoes and mint pesto, but pheasant (or fingerling potatoes) are not available at my market—so I made something else." Don't limit, improvise. Instead of pheasant, certainly duck or even chicken would work. And although of a different shape, small red bliss or Yukon Gold potatoes would be excellent substitutes for the fingerlings.

Virtually hundreds of salads and options can be created from the base of thirty main course salads and sixty variations in *Salad Days*. Serve Roasted Root Vegetable Slaw (page 177) rather than the Grilled Vegetables on the Marinated French Lentils (page 85). And while you're at it, rather than Walnut Oil Vinaigrette for the Marinated French Lentils salad, substitute Rosemary Vinaigrette from the White Bean Salad (page 73). Choose almost any of the sixty variations to accompany your salad, and you have mothered an entirely different salad. A veritable mix and match, *Salad Days* can be your primer for creative cooking.

K E E P   I T   C L E A N

Improperly handled or prepared foods can cause myriad problems, from spoiled and wasted food to food-borne illness. Use good sense when handling food. Always wash your hands before, during, and after handling food. Cross-contamination is a nemesis that must be seriously attended to in the kitchen. That means sanitizing hands and equipment after a specific food is handled. After preparing raw chicken, always sanitize and thoroughly clean cutting boards, knives, other equipment, and hands before moving on to vegetables.

Cross-contamination can also occur if an unwashed fruit or vegetable is handled immediately before handling another food without hand and equipment sanitation between the two. Before cutting, wash fruits and vegetables with cool water (never use soap because it would be absorbed by the food); otherwise, dirt and bacteria can be spread from the unwashed outer surface to the edible interior. So keep it clean and stay healthy.

Ingredients and Essential Recipes

The American market basket of fresh seasonal produce is second to none in the world. This wasn't always the case. In the mid 60s, as a nineteen-year-old just out of The Culinary Institute of America and working in clubs, restaurants, and hotels in New York City, I would typically reach for a can if a recipe called for such foods as sorrel, salsify, celery root, or wild mushrooms. Today, fresh markets abound, providing both professional cooks and home cooks with an extraordinary array of fresh ingredients.

It's an exciting time for cooking. Whether you are shopping at the Farmers Market at Union Square in New York City or the James City Farmers Market on Strawberry Plains Road in Williamsburg, Virginia, you can fill your basket with juicy ripe fruit, lushly green herbs, nose-tingling radishes, earthy mushrooms, crisp vegetables, aromatic flowers, unadulterated dairy products, and much more. Produce from such markets will woo and satisfy your senses, and at the same time you'll support the small farmers and intrepid foragers who are making the time you spend in the kitchen rewarding and delicious.

FRESH HERBS

I cannot imagine cooking without fresh herbs. In fact, virtually all the thirty main course salads in *Salad Days* contain at least one fresh herb. Fresh herbs are like the frosting on the cake; foods can be delicious without herbs (many cakes are compelling before being frosted), but their inclusion in a recipe heightens other flavors as well as infuses additional dimensions of flavor (almost any cake becomes a dulcet delectation when bathed with ganache). Used with a subtle touch, herbs can create gastronomic alchemy.

I disagree, however, with the school of thought that herbs eliminate the need for salt. A light sprinkle of salt is nature's way of releasing flavors from good ingredients. Salt becomes the demon only when it camouflages bad ingredients or processed foods, providing the major flavor component.

We are fortunate to cook at a time when the most commonly used fresh herbs are available year-round. The motivated cook has few reasons to use dried herbs (though being holed up in a mountain cabin with several feet of snow on the ground is a good one). If you must use dried herbs, do so with a very light hand. Dried herbs have a more aggressive flavor that can introduce bitterness or overwhelm a recipe.

The following is a list of the fresh herbs used in *Salad Days*. I have starred the herbs that appear in more than six recipes.

basil*	marjoram
chives*	mint
cilantro (a.k.a. coriander and Chinese parsley)	oregano*
	rosemary*
curly parsley*	sage
dill	tarragon
Italian parsley	thyme*

At Ganache Hill I enjoy the convenience of picking fresh herbs for most of the year from an herb garden just outside my front door. My garden was designed and planted by Audrey Julian, owner of the Dilworthtown Country Store in the historic village of Dilworthtown in West Chester, Pennsylvania. Besides running the oldest continuously operated country store in the United States, Audrey is an inveterate gardener specializing in herbs. I met Audrey at the Nancy Thomas Gallery in Yorktown, Virginia, on a gorgeous spring day when she sold her herb plants as part of the gallery's annual spring show.

My friend, artist, and co-conspirator on *An Alphabet of Sweets,* Nancy suggested that Audrey transform the earth around Ganache Hill into an herbal idyll. And indeed she did. After advising on the preparation of the soil (one-third dirt, one-third sand, and one-third peat moss), Audrey transported dozens of plants to Williamsburg from Dilworthtown, then planted the herbs to maximize growth and minimize maintenance. The results are an enchanting space that is both practical and beautiful.

Although I am lucky to have the space for so many plants, I would encourage anyone with a passion for fresh herbs but limited geography to dedicate a planter or window box to a few hearty herbs such as rosemary, thyme, and sage. Believe me, picking your own fresh herbs for a salad, soup, or quick sauté is much more rewarding than sprinkling dried leaves from a bottle.

THE DRY PANTRY

Organizing the ingredients for a meal can seem daunting. While I am a proponent of market shopping (that is, purchasing fresh foods to be used that day), a cook's life can become more enjoyable when boxed, canned, bottled, dried, and preserved foods and other cooking necessities are on hand.

The following list of foods, all used to some degree in *Salad Days,* can be purchased in most well-stocked supermarkets. Since your kitchen, like mine, may lack sufficient storage to hold all these items, I have starred products that are used more often in this book. Stock these staples, and you can get cooking sooner than later!

Beans and Grains

arborio rice

basmati rice

black turtle beans

brown rice

couscous

French green lentils

garbanzo beans

pearl barley

quinoa

wheat berries

white beans

white grits (stone-ground)

wild rice

Cooking Oils

corn oil

extra-virgin olive oil *

peanut oil *

safflower oil *

sesame oil

vegetable oil *

walnut oil

Dried Herbs, Seeds, and Spices

bay leaves

black peppercorns *

cayenne pepper (ground) *

celery seeds

cinnamon (ground)

cumin (ground)

curry powder

dry mustard

poppy seeds

pumpkin seeds

saffron

sesame seeds

Szechuan peppercorns

white pepper (ground)

Miscellaneous Flavorings

blackstrap molasses

brown mustard

chili oil

Dijon-style mustard*

honey*

hot sauce * (I use Tabasco)

Key lime juice

Meaux mustard

soy sauce *

Nuts

almonds

cashews

hazelnuts

peanuts *

pecans

pine nuts

walnuts*

Vinegars

balsamic

cider *

red raspberry *

red wine *

rice wine *

sherry wine

white wine

Staples

active dry yeast

all-purpose flour *

baking powder

baking soda

cornstarch

cream of tartar

granulated sugar *

iodized salt *

kosher salt

masa harina (corn flour)

mayonnaise*

peanut butter

raisins

yellow cornmeal

Wines, Spirits, and Beer for Cooking

beer

bourbon

brandy

chardonnay

crème de cassis

dark beer

dry sherry

dry vermouth

dry white wine *

gin

port wine

rice wine

sauvignon blanc

sour mash whiskey

tequila

zinfandel

&

*T*he Trellis Barbecue Sauce

Yields 2 cups

1 tablespoon vegetable oil

1½ cups finely diced onion

¾ cup finely diced green bell pepper

½ cup finely diced carrot

1¼ cups chopped tomato

½ cup tomato juice

¼ cup cider vinegar

¼ cup ketchup

¼ cup molasses

1 tablespoon hot sauce

1½ teaspoons salt

Equipment

measuring spoons
measuring cups
paring knife
cook's knife
cutting board
vegetable peeler
3-quart saucepan
metal kitchen spoon
immersion blender or
   food processor fitted
   with a metal blade
medium-gauge strainer
3-quart stainless steel bowl
instant-read test
   thermometer
plastic wrap

Heat the vegetable oil in a 3-quart saucepan over medium heat. When the oil is hot, add the onion, green bell pepper, and carrot. Cook, stirring frequently, until tender, about 10 minutes. Add the tomato and cook for 5 more minutes. Add the tomato juice, cider vinegar, ketchup, molasses, hot sauce, and salt. Bring to a boil, then adjust the heat and allow the mixture to simmer, stirring occasionally, for 30 minutes.

Remove the saucepan from the heat, then puree the mixture using a handheld immersion blender or a food processor fitted with a metal blade. Strain the puree through a medium-gauge strainer into a 3-quart stainless steel bowl.

Cool the barbecue sauce in an ice water bath to a temperature of 40 to 45 degrees Fahrenheit. Cover with plastic wrap and refrigerate for 24 hours before using. (The flavor of the sauce will be enhanced during this time.) The sauce may be stored in a covered, noncorrosive container in the refrigerator for several days.

The Chef's Touch

The Trellis Barbecue Sauce was conceived by one of our former assistant chefs, Chet Flanagan. Chet was not only a great cook, but he also had a flair for "down-home-style" soups and sauces.

First prepared by Chet for a Trellis employee picnic, this sauce was highly praised for its tasteful attitude (mellow heat and big flavor). The first appearance of the sauce on The Trellis dinner menu was with Grilled Gulf Shrimp with Crispy Grits Cake in December 1989. Although Chet moved on in the spring of 1995, he left this barbecue sauce as a tasty legacy to his finely tuned cooking skills.

🦎

Saffron-Infused White Wine Vinegar

Yields ¼ cup

¼ cup white wine vinegar   small pinch saffron (about ½ gram)

Heat the white wine vinegar in a 1½-quart saucepan over medium-high heat. Remove the vinegar from the heat as soon as it begins to simmer, add the saffron, and stir to incorporate. Steep the saffron in the vinegar for 1½ to 2 hours, or as long as a few days before using. For extended storage, place the infused vinegar in a covered, noncorrosive container in the refrigerator until ready to use.

Equipment

measuring cups
1½-quart noncorrosive
   saucepan

The Chef's Touch

This recipe yields the amount of vinegar needed to prepare the Saffron Vinaigrette (see page 136), but don't hesitate to make more. A splash or two of flavored vinegar on a piece of fish or chicken during the cooking process is certain to yield delicious and tangy eating.

Many other flavored vinegars may be easily produced (or purchased if you're more flush than industrious). I am particularly fond of vinegars infused with fresh herbs. Whatever herb you choose to infuse in the vinegar, utilize a good-quality white wine vinegar. Heat the vinegar to a simmer, then pour over cleaned herbs that have been placed in a noncorrosive container. Allow the vinegar to cool to room temperature before tightly covering the container. Set aside at room temperature for 2 to 3 weeks, until the vinegar has been infused with the flavor of the herbs, and strain before using. The infused vinegars may be stored in the tightly sealed noncorrosive container in the refrigerator for 2 to 3 months.

🔏

Vegetable Stock

Yields about 5 cups

1½ quarts plus 2 tablespoons cold water
2 tablespoons safflower oil
1 large onion (about 3/4 pound), peeled and chopped
1 medium leek (about 8 ounces), root end and green top removed, cut in half lengthwise, rinsed under cold running water, and chopped
1 medium tomato (about 6 ounces), washed, cored, and chopped

1 medium carrot (about 4 ounces), peeled, ends trimmed, and chopped
2 stalks celery (about 4 ounces), ends trimmed, washed, and chopped
2 teaspoons salt
2 to 3 sprigs fresh parsley
¼ teaspoon crushed whole black peppercorns

Equipment

measuring cups
measuring spoons
paring knife
cook's knife
cutting board
vegetable peeler
5-quart saucepan
metal kitchen spoon
medium-gauge strainer
3-quart stainless steel bowl
instant-read test
   thermometer
plastic wrap

Heat 2 tablespoons of water and the safflower oil in a 5-quart saucepan over medium-high heat. When the water and oil mixture is hot, add the onion, leek, tomato, carrot, celery, and salt. Cook, stirring occasionally, for 6 minutes.

Add the remaining 1½ quarts of water, parsley sprigs, and peppercorns. Bring to a boil, then adjust the heat and allow to simmer for 1 hour, until the stock has a pleasant vegetal flavor.

Strain the stock through a medium-gauge strainer into a 3-quart stainless steel bowl. Cool the stock in an ice water bath to a temperature of 40 to 45 degrees Fahrenheit. Cover the cold stock with plastic wrap and refrigerate for up to 3 days before using.

The Chef's Touch

This recipe produces a subtly flavored and lightly colored stock—just right for the recipes in *Salad Days* calling for vegetable stock. For more intensely flavored stocks, use more assertively flavored vegetables such as fennel, herbs, and even shiitake mushrooms. Keep in mind that these vegetables, herbs, and mushrooms will not only intensify the flavor but may significantly darken the color of the finished stock. This may not be desirable with certain recipes, such as Warm Grits Cake (see page 161).

*F*resh Herb Vinaigrette

Yields 1½ cups

4 tablespoons white wine vinegar

2 tablespoons fresh lemon juice

1 cup extra-virgin olive oil

2 tablespoons chopped fresh Italian parsley

1½ tablespoons chopped fresh chives

1 tablespoon chopped fresh thyme

2 teaspoons chopped fresh tarragon

1 teaspoon salt

¼ teaspoon freshly ground black pepper

In a 3-quart stainless steel bowl, whisk together the white wine vinegar and lemon juice. Add the olive oil in a slow, steady stream while whisking, until it is fully incorporated. Add the parsley, chives, thyme, and tarragon, and whisk to combine. Add the salt and pepper, and whisk to combine. Cover with plastic wrap and set aside at room temperature until needed, up to several hours, or refrigerate in a covered, noncorrosive container for 1 to 2 days. If refrigerated, return the vinaigrette to room temperature and whisk vigorously before using.

Equipment

measuring spoons
measuring cups
cook's knife
cutting board
3-quart stainless steel bowl
whisk
plastic wrap

The Chef's Touch

This multipurpose vinaigrette has the perfect balance of acidity and flavor to complement many of the salads in *Salad Days*. I have used it in place of the Rosemary Vinaigrette in the White Bean Salad (see page 73), or if you are not a garlic lover, use it in place of the Roasted Garlic Dressing to dress the Warm Grilled Eggplant, Scallions, and Plum Tomatoes salad (see page 113). Or just toss with your favorite greens and let your palate savor this uncomplicated but delicious amalgam.

※

*B*lue Cheese Dressing

Yields 2¹/₄ cups

2 tablespoons white wine vinegar
³/₄ cup mayonnaise
¹/₂ cup sour cream

1 teaspoon fresh lemon juice
ground white pepper to taste
4 ounces blue cheese, crumbled

Equipment

measuring spoons
measuring cup
3-quart stainless steel bowl
whisk
rubber spatula
plastic wrap

In a 3-quart stainless steel bowl, whisk the white wine vinegar, mayonnaise, sour cream, and lemon juice until smooth. Season with pepper and whisk to combine. Add the blue cheese and use a rubber spatula to stir until incorporated. Cover the dressing with plastic wrap and refrigerate until ready to serve, up to 3 days.

The Chef's Touch

Because I am allergic to blue mold cheeses, I cannot partake of this sensuous dressing, but I hope you do not suffer the same fate and can add this to your repertoire of dressings.

※

*R*oasted Shallot Dressing

Yields 1¹/₄ cups

6 whole shallots (about 6 ounces), unpeeled
³/₄ cup plus 1 tablespoon extra-virgin olive
    oil
salt and freshly ground black pepper to taste
2 tablespoons sherry wine vinegar

2 tablespoons white wine vinegar
2 teaspoons chopped fresh tarragon
¹/₂ teaspoon kosher salt
¹/₈ teaspoon ground white pepper

Preheat the oven to 325 degrees Fahrenheit.

Cut the shallots into quarters. Place the shallots on a pie tin, sprinkle with 1 tablespoon of olive oil, and lightly season with salt and pepper. Cover the pie tin with aluminum foil and roast the shallots in the preheated oven for 30 minutes, until golden brown and tender. Remove the shallots from the oven and allow to cool at room temperature, covered, for 30 minutes.

Trim the root ends and remove and discard the skins from the shallots. Cut the shallots into thin strips and then set them aside at room temperature until needed.

In the bowl of a food processor fitted with a metal blade, process the sherry wine vinegar, white wine vinegar, the remaining ¾ cup of olive oil, and half of the roasted shallots for 30 seconds. Transfer the mixture to a 3-quart stainless steel bowl. Add the remaining shallots, tarragon, kosher salt, and the white pepper, and whisk to combine. Cover with plastic wrap and set aside at room temperature until needed, up to several hours, or refrigerate in a covered, noncorrosive container up to 3 days. If refrigerated, return the dressing to room temperature and whisk vigorously before using.

Equipment
measuring cup
measuring spoons
cook's knife
cutting board
pie tin
aluminum foil
food processor with metal blade
rubber spatula
3-quart stainless steel bowl
whisk
plastic wrap

The Chef's Touch

This dressing debuted at The Trellis in the fall of 1985 along with a salad of arugula, Belgian endive, and red Bartlett pears. Since then, roasted shallot dressing has appeared often on the menu, most recently with a salad of fingerling potatoes with a grilled peppered tuna steak as a main course selection. Because of its versatility I include it here, although it is not used specifically with any recipes in *Salad Days*. I think you will find it a delightful substitute for many of the listed dressings and vinaigrettes.

*T*he Trellis Vinaigrette

Yields 2 cups

6 tablespoons cider vinegar
3 tablespoons fresh lemon juice
4 teaspoons Dijon-style mustard

1 teaspoon salt
¼ teaspoon freshly ground black pepper
1½ cups safflower oil

In a 3-quart stainless steel bowl, whisk together the vinegar, lemon juice, mustard, salt, and pepper. Add the safflower oil in a slow, steady stream while whisking until it is fully incorporated. Cover with plastic wrap and set aside at room temperature until needed, up to several hours, or refrigerate in a covered, noncorrosive container for sev-

Equipment
measuring spoons
measuring cups
3-quart stainless steel bowl
whisk
plastic wrap

eral days. If refrigerated, return the vinaigrette to room temperature and whisk vigorously before using.

The Chef's Touch

After dressing every luncheon side salad at The Trellis for more than eighteen years (over 1.5 million salads!), The Trellis Vinaigrette continues to be one of the most frequently requested recipes. Although included in *The Trellis Cookbook,* I would feel awfully stingy not to include it in *Salad Days.* So if you need to dress up just about any combination of greens, try this one.

Greens

Sliced Beets with Curly Endive, Red Bliss Potato Salad, Honey Mustard Roasted Walnuts, and Meaux Mustard Vinaigrette

Serves 4

Meaux Mustard Vinaigrette

2 tablespoons red wine vinegar

2 tablespoons Moutarde de Meaux Pommery mustard

¾ cup extra-virgin olive oil

½ cup safflower oil

salt and freshly ground black pepper to taste

Red Bliss Potato Salad

3 pounds red bliss potatoes, washed but not peeled

salt and freshly ground black pepper to taste

1 medium red onion (about 6 ounces), peeled and thinly sliced

2 tablespoons fresh chopped parsley

Meaux Mustard Vinaigrette

Honey Mustard Roasted Walnuts

1 tablespoon unsalted butter

1 tablespoon honey

1 tablespoon Moutarde de Meaux Pommery mustard

1 cup walnuts

salt to taste

Salad Greens and Beets

5 to 6 small beets (about 1 pound), stems trimmed to ¼ inch

¾ pound curly endive, cored, trimmed, cut into ¾-inch pieces, washed, and dried

MAKE THE MEAUX MUSTARD VINAIGRETTE

In a 3-quart stainless steel bowl, whisk together the red wine vinegar and Meaux mustard until combined. Add the olive oil in a slow, steady stream while whisking until incorporated, followed by the safflower oil, still whisking until combined. Add salt and pepper, and whisk to combine. Cover tightly with plastic wrap and set aside at room temperature until needed.

PREPARE THE RED BLISS POTATO SALAD

Place the potatoes in a 6-quart saucepan and cover with cold water. Bring to a simmer over medium-high heat, then adjust the heat to simmer slowly until the potatoes are cooked through, about 20 to 22 minutes. Drain the hot water from the potatoes, then cool them in the saucepan under running cold water. Thoroughly drain the potatoes in a colander. Cut the potatoes into 1-inch cubes and transfer to a 7-quart stainless steel bowl. Season with salt and pepper. Add the onion and parsley and toss to combine. Vigorously whisk the Meaux mustard vinaigrette, then add ¾ cup to the potatoes. (Cover the remaining ¾ cup with plastic wrap and set aside at room temperature until needed.) Use a rubber spatula to combine the ingredients until the potatoes and onions are coated with the vinaigrette. Set aside at room temperature, loosely covered with plastic wrap, for up to 2 hours before serving. Or cool to room temperature and then refrigerate in a covered, noncorrosive container for up to 2 days before serving.

MAKE THE HONEY MUSTARD ROASTED WALNUTS

Preheat the oven to 325 degrees Fahrenheit.

Heat the butter in a small nonstick sauté pan over medium heat. When the butter is melted and hot, remove from the heat, add the honey and mustard, and whisk to combine. Add the walnuts to the hot honey mustard mixture. Use a rubber spatula to combine until the walnuts are evenly coated with the mixture. Transfer the walnuts to a nonstick baking sheet. Use a rubber spatula to separate and spread the nuts. Place the baking sheet in the preheated oven for 12 minutes. Remove from the oven and season with salt. Cool the walnuts to room temperature. Keep at room temperature in a tightly sealed plastic container until needed.

FINISH AND ASSEMBLE THE SALAD

Heat 2 quarts of lightly salted water in a 3-quart saucepan over medium-high heat. When the water boils, add the beets and cook for 20 minutes. The texture of the cooked beets should be very firm. Transfer the cooked beets to ice water to cool.

Peel and slice the beets about ⅛ inch thick. (This can be done by hand with a sharp cook's knife or use a mandoline.)

Arrange enough beet slices to form a ring around the outside edge of 4 room-temperature 10- to 12-inch plates; the slices should slightly overlap each other. Place an equal amount of curly endive pieces in the center of each plate, being careful not to cover the beets. Vigorously whisk the vinaigrette. Sprinkle each portion of curly endive with 3 tablespoons of vinaigrette. Spoon an equal amount of red bliss potato salad on the greens on each plate. Top each salad with some of the roasted walnuts. Serve immediately.

¥

*W*alnut-Crusted Striped Bass Variation

½ cup finely chopped walnuts

2 tablespoons Moutarde de Meaux Pommery mustard

2 tablespoons chopped fresh parsley

1 tablespoon extra-virgin olive oil

4 6-ounce skinless striped bass (rockfish) fillets

salt and freshly ground black pepper to taste

Preheat the oven to broil.

In a 1-quart stainless steel bowl, use a rubber spatula to combine the walnuts, mustard, parsley, and olive oil.

Place the fish fillets on a nonstick baking sheet. Season with salt and pepper. Spoon 2 level tablespoons of the walnut mixture on each fillet and use your fingers to spread and coat each fillet with the mixture. Place the baking sheet in the preheated oven and broil the fish for 5 minutes, until golden brown. Lower the oven temperature to 300 degrees Fahrenheit and cook the fillets for 5 more minutes. Remove the fillets from the oven. Place a striped bass fillet on each salad. Serve immediately.

ॐ

Honey Duck Stir-Fry Variation

2 tablespoons honey
2 tablespoons red wine vinegar
4 ounces lean hickory smoked bacon, cut into ¼-inch dice
4 3-ounce boneless, skinless duck breasts, cut into strips 4 inches long and ¼ inch thick

salt and freshly ground black pepper to taste
1 bunch scallions, cleaned, trimmed, and cut into 3-inch-long pieces, then quartered lengthwise

In a 1-quart bowl, whisk together the honey and red wine vinegar. Set aside.

Heat a large nonstick sauté pan or wok over high heat. When hot, add the bacon and stir-fry until browned and crisp, about 3 to 4 minutes. Transfer the bacon to a baking sheet lined with paper towels to drain. Wipe the excess fat from the pan. Return the pan to the heat for 5 minutes, until very hot. Place the duck breasts in the hot pan, season with salt and pepper, and stir-fry until browned, about 2 to 3 minutes. Add the scallions and stir-fry for 30 seconds. Add the honey and vinegar mixture, and cook for 45 seconds. Remove from the heat and mix in the bacon. Use a slotted kitchen spoon to place an equal amount of stir-fry on each salad. Serve immediately.

The Chef's Touch

MY FONDNESS for beets does not extend to their green leafy tops (unless they are quite young and home-grown). The inherently pungent and acidic leaves often suffer during transit and storage, making them even less appealing by the time they get to market. On the other hand, the ruby-colored beet root is the jewel beneath the crown. Capable of a multitude of transit and storage abuse, the startling color of the beet, as well as its boldly sweet taste, is one of nature's marvels.

The textural Moutarde de Meaux Pommery (a French grain mustard) adds a deliciously distinctive flavor to our vinaigrette. If you are not able to locate this mustard, substitute another high-quality grain mustard.

The Chef's Touch

The Meaux Mustard Vinaigrette recipe yields 1½ cups. Keep the vinaigrette at room temperature for 2 to 3 hours before using or refrigerate it in a covered, noncorrosive container for 2 to 3 days. If refrigerated, return the vinaigrette to room temperature and whisk vigorously before using.

After toasting, the Honey Mustard Roasted Walnuts can be kept at room temperature for several days in a tightly sealed plastic container.

One medium head of curly endive, about ¾ pound as purchased, should yield ½ pound of prepared greens. For crisp greens, spin-dry the washed curly endive pieces in a salad spinner.

In New England we called it striped bass, and here in Virginia it's rockfish. Either way, it makes for spirited fishing and luscious eating. Whether filleted and then grilled or broiled, or stuffed with shrimp and served whole (which was a specialty years ago when I worked for the Colonial Williamsburg Foundation), rockfish/striped bass has a firm texture and mild flavor. Sadly overfished and unavailable in many areas, striped bass is now becoming available at certain times of the year. Farm-raised striped bass, although expensive, is of excellent quality and readily available year-round.

Chicken is a perfect replacement in the stir-fry recipe if duck is unavailable.

I'll take my cue from the French mustard and suggest a red French wine to savor with this salad. Consider a young and exuberant beaujolais. A recent vintage Fleurie with mellow tannins and rich fruit flavor would be an excellent choice indeed.

Fennel and Watercress with Ratatouille and Roasted Tomato Vinaigrette

Roasted Tomato Vinaigrette

6 medium plum tomatoes (about 2 ounces each), washed and cored
salt and freshly ground black pepper to taste

$^3/_4$ cup extra-virgin olive oil
$^1/_4$ cup red wine vinegar
1 teaspoon chopped fresh thyme

Ratatouille

2 cloves garlic, unpeeled
$^1/_4$ cup plus 2 tablespoons extra-virgin olive oil
salt and freshly ground black pepper to taste
1 medium red onion (about 6 ounces), sliced
1 large zucchini (about $^3/_4$ pound), washed and cut into sticks 3 inches long and $^1/_2$ inch thick
1 medium yellow squash (about $^1/_2$ pound), washed and cut into sticks 3 inches long and $^1/_2$ inch thick

1 small eggplant (about $^3/_4$ pound), washed and cut into sticks 3 inches long and $^1/_2$ inch thick
1 large tomato (about $^3/_4$ pound), peeled, seeded, and cut into $^1/_2$-inch cubes
1 tablespoon chopped fresh basil
$^1/_2$ tablespoon chopped fresh thyme

Salad Greens and Garnish

$^1/_2$ cup pine nuts
$^1/_2$ tablespoon fresh lemon juice
1 large fennel bulb (about 1 pound)

$^1/_2$ pound watercress, trimmed, washed, and dried

MAKE THE
ROASTED TOMATO VINAIGRETTE
Preheat the oven to 225 degrees Fahrenheit.

Cut each plum tomato in half lengthwise, then cut each half into 3 sections lengthwise. Place the tomato sections, skin side down and evenly spaced, on a baking sheet lined with parchment paper. Season lightly with salt and pepper. Place the tomatoes in the preheated oven and roast for 3 hours. Remove from the oven and allow to cool to room temperature. Chop the tomatoes into ¼-inch pieces. In a 3-quart stainless steel bowl, vigorously whisk together the olive oil with the red wine vinegar. Add the tomatoes and thyme, and stir to combine. Adjust the seasoning, cover tightly with plastic wrap, and set aside at room temperature until needed.

PREPARE THE RATATOUILLE
Preheat the oven to 325 degrees Fahrenheit.

Place the garlic in a pie tin or small baking dish, sprinkle with ½ tablespoon of olive oil, and then lightly season with salt and pepper. Cover the pie tin with aluminum foil. Place in the preheated oven and roast the garlic until tender, about 30 minutes. Remove the garlic from the oven, discard the aluminum foil, and cool to room temperature. When the garlic is cool enough to handle, peel and trim the cloves or use your fingers to squeeze the pulp away from the skin, and then finely chop the pulp.

Heat 1½ tablespoons of olive oil in a large nonstick sauté pan over medium heat. When hot, add the red onion, lightly season with salt and pepper, and sauté for 2 minutes, until tender. Add the roasted garlic, zucchini, and yellow squash. Lightly season with salt and pepper, and sauté for 3 minutes, stirring frequently. Add the eggplant, lightly season with salt and pepper, and sauté for 2 minutes. Add the tomato cubes, basil, and thyme, and toss to combine. Remove from the heat and transfer the mixture to a 7-quart stainless steel bowl. Add the remaining ¼ cup of olive oil and stir to combine. Adjust the seasoning with salt and pepper. Cover tightly with plastic wrap and set aside at room temperature for 1 to 2 hours before serving.

Equipment

paring knife
measuring cup
measuring spoons
cook's knife
cutting board
5-quart saucepan
salad spinner
baking sheet
parchment paper
two 3-quart stainless steel
   bowls
whisk
plastic wrap
pie tin
aluminum foil
large nonstick sauté pan
7-quart bowl
colander

*Smoked shrimp variation
   requires:*
smoker
basting brush
paper towels

*Monkfish variation
   requires:*
nonstick baking sheet
   with sides
slotted spoon

FINISH AND ASSEMBLE THE SALAD

Preheat the oven to 325 degrees Fahrenheit.

Toast the pine nuts on a baking sheet in the preheated oven for 10 minutes. Remove the nuts from the oven and set aside at room temperature until needed.

In a 3-quart stainless steel bowl, combine 2 cups of cold water with the lemon juice. Wash, core, and cut the fennel bulb into very thin strips and immediately place in the acidulated water. (This will help prevent any discoloration as well as crisp the fennel.)

Divide and arrange the watercress, stem ends toward the center, in a ring near the outside edge of four 10- to 12-inch room-temperature plates. Drain the fennel in a colander, rinse under cold running water, and shake dry. Divide and arrange the fennel over the center area of each plate. Whisk the vinaigrette. Dress the watercress and fennel strips on each plate with 2 to 3 tablespoons of the vinaigrette. Place an equal amount of ratatouille on the center of each salad. Dress the ratatouille with 2 to 3 tablespoons of the vinaigrette. Sprinkle 2 tablespoons of pine nuts over each salad. Serve immediately.

✳

Smoked Shrimp Variation

½ cup warm water
¼ cup kosher salt
2 tablespoons granulated sugar
½ cup cool water

1¼ pounds large shrimp, peeled and
  deveined
½ tablespoon olive oil

Prepare the brine in a 3-quart stainless steel bowl by combining the warm water, kosher salt, and sugar. Whisk to dissolve the salt and sugar. Add the cool water and stir to combine. Immerse the shrimp in the brine for 3 to 4 *seconds*. Remove and pat dry with paper towels.

Line the top shelf of a smoker with parchment paper. Brush the parchment paper with the olive oil. Place the shrimp on the shelf in the smoker and smoke for 45 minutes.

Remove the shrimp from the smoker. Divide the shrimp into 4 portions and place on top of each salad. Serve immediately.

*O*ven-Roasted Monkfish

2 pounds thoroughly trimmed monkfish
  fillet, cut into 2-inch pieces
2 tablespoons dry white wine
1 tablespoon fresh lemon juice

1 tablespoon extra-virgin olive oil
salt and freshly ground black pepper to taste
1 teaspoon chopped fresh thyme

Preheat the oven to 350 degrees Fahrenheit.

Place the monkfish pieces in a 3-quart stainless steel bowl and sprinkle with the white wine, lemon juice, and olive oil. Season with salt and pepper. Sprinkle on the thyme and toss to coat. Cook immediately or cover with plastic wrap and refrigerate until ready to use (up to 24 hours).

Use a slotted spoon to transfer the monkfish from the marinade to a nonstick baking sheet with sides. Place in the preheated oven and roast for 15 to 20 minutes, until cooked through. Remove the monkfish from the oven and use a slotted spoon to remove the pieces from the baking sheet. Divide the monkfish among the salads. Serve immediately or place the monkfish in a preheated 200-degree Fahrenheit oven to keep warm for 15 to 20 minutes.

The Chef's Touch

T H E   F I R S T   time I tasted an oven-roasted tomato was in 1985 in Florence, Italy, during a cooking course taught by the esteemed historian and culinarian Giuliano Bugialli. I marveled at the opulent sweetness that remained after the tomato's tasteless water was drawn out by hours of low-temperature roasting. Amazed that such a simple technique was not conventionally used in America, I lost no time roasting tomatoes when I returned to Williamsburg and The Trellis.

(*continued on next page*)

The Chef's Touch

The Roasted Tomato Vinaigrette recipe yields about 2¼ cups. The vinaigrette may be kept at room temperature for several hours before using or refrigerated in a covered, noncorrosive container for 2 to 3 days. If refrigerated, return the vinaigrette to room temperature and whisk vigorously before using.

Roasted tomatoes may be used in pasta dishes, stir-fries, or just about anywhere you want a concentrated sweet tomato flavor. After roasting, cool the tomatoes to room temperature, then store in a tightly sealed plastic container in the refrigerator for several days. Some cooks cover the roasted tomatoes with oil to increase the length of storage, but I feel the oil detracts from their explicit sweetness.

One large bunch of watercress, about ½ pound, should yield ¼ pound, trimmed (cut away about ½ inch of the stem ends), washed, and dried leaves. For crisp greens, spin-dry the washed watercress in a salad spinner.

Since watercress is very perishable, purchase only as much as needed and keep the stem ends iced in the refrigerator until ready to use.

After smoking the shrimp, cool them to room temperature and use immediately or store in a tightly sealed plastic container in the refrigerator for 1 or 2 days. Our quick method of curing and smoking gives flavor to the shrimp but does not preserve them like the commercial process.

If smoking the shrimp proves impractical, then consider sautéed shrimp. Heat 1 tablespoon of extra-virgin olive oil in a large nonstick sauté pan over medium-high heat. When hot, add the shrimp, season lightly with salt and freshly ground black pepper, and sauté for 4 to 5 minutes.

Be certain that you or your fishmonger (does anyone *really* know a fish-*monger?*) is dutiful about trimming the tough membrane away from the monkfish, and you'll be rewarded with a tender fish beneath. Monkfish sometimes gets a bad rap for tough texture because of improper handling.

We tested this recipe at Ganache Hill on a dreary winter day, so I brightened my spirits by pairing the salad with a glass of Hanna, Sonoma County, Chardonnay. The wine had just the right amount of fruit, neither too elegant nor too austere, to pair with the mélange of Mediterranean flavors.

Romaine Lettuce, Granny Smith Apples, Toasted Hazelnuts, and New York State Cheddar Cheese with Sherry Wine Dressing

Serves 4

Sherry Wine Dressing

½ cup whole hazelnuts
2½ tablespoons sherry wine vinegar

¾ cup safflower oil
salt and freshly ground black pepper to taste

Salad Greens and Garnish

½ cup whole hazelnuts
½ tablespoon fresh lemon juice
2 Granny Smith apples, unpeeled
1½ pounds romaine lettuce, cored, cut
   widthwise into ½-inch pieces, washed,
   and dried

½ pound New York State sharp cheddar
   cheese, cut into sticks 2¾ inches long
   and ¼ inch thick

❧

MAKE THE SHERRY WINE DRESSING
Preheat the oven to 325 degrees Fahrenheit.

Toast the hazelnuts on a baking sheet with sides in the preheated oven for 20 to 25 minutes. Remove them from the oven and immediately cover with a damp towel. Invert another baking sheet over the first one to hold in the steam (this makes the nuts easier to skin). After 5 minutes, remove the skins from the nuts by placing small quantities inside a folded dry towel and rubbing vigorously between your hands. Cool the nuts thoroughly before processing in the bowl of a food processor fitted with a metal blade for

Equipment

measuring cup
measuring spoons
cook's knife
cutting board
salad spinner
2 baking sheets with sides
2 large 100 percent cotton
  towels
food processor with metal
  blade
two 3-quart stainless steel
  bowls
whisk
handheld immersion
  blender
plastic wrap
colander

Burger variation requires:
small nonstick sauté pan
5-quart stainless steel bowl
charcoal grill
spatula

Quail variation requires:
large nonstick sauté pan
paring knife
charcoal grill
spatula

30 seconds, until finely ground. Transfer the ground hazelnuts to a 3-quart stainless steel bowl. Add the sherry wine vinegar and whisk to combine. Add the safflower oil and whisk until blended. Season with salt and pepper. Use a handheld immersion blender or a food processor to blend the dressing until fairly smooth and emulsified. Cover with plastic wrap and set aside at room temperature until needed.

FINISH AND ASSEMBLE THE SALAD
Preheat the oven to 325 degrees Fahrenheit.

Toast and skin the hazelnuts as previously described for the dressing. Cool the nuts to room temperature before cutting each in half. Set aside until needed.

In a 3-quart stainless steel bowl, add the lemon juice to 2 cups of cold water. Core and quarter the apples, then slice each quarter lengthwise into ¼-inch-thick slices and immediately place in the acidulated water to prevent oxidation (brown discoloration).

Divide and arrange the romaine pieces on four 10- to 12-inch room-temperature plates. Drain the apples in a colander, rinse under cold running water, and shake dry. Arrange the apple slices around the lettuce, with the skin side touching or near the edge of the plate. Whisk the dressing. Dress the romaine and apples on each plate with 2 tablespoons of dressing. Sprinkle the cheddar cheese and hazelnuts on the center of each salad. Drizzle 1 to 2 tablespoons of the dressing over the cheese and hazelnuts. Serve immediately.

*G*rilled *Veal Burger Variation*

½ tablespoon extra-virgin olive oil	salt and freshly ground black pepper to taste
6 tablespoons finely chopped shallots	1 pound ground veal
½ teaspoon chopped fresh sage	3 ounces pork fat, diced
½ teaspoon chopped fresh rosemary	

Heat the olive oil in a medium nonstick sauté pan over medium heat. When hot, add the shallots and sauté until lightly browned, about 6 minutes. Add the sage and rosemary, and season with salt and pepper. Place the mixture in a 9- to 10-inch dish, uncovered, in the refrigerator to cool.

In a 5-quart stainless steel bowl, gently but thoroughly combine the ground veal, pork fat, and cooled shallot and herb mixture.

Gently form the meat mixture into four 5-ounce burgers 1 inch thick. Cover the burgers with plastic wrap and refrigerate until needed (up to 24 hours).

Preheat the oven to 300 degrees Fahrenheit.

Season the burgers with salt and pepper.

Grill the burgers over a medium wood or charcoal fire for 4 minutes on each side.

(The veal burgers may also be cooked on a well-seasoned flat griddle or in a large nonstick sauté pan over medium-high heat. Cook for about the same amount of time as listed for grilling.) Remove the burgers from the grill. Place the veal burgers in the preheated oven and cook until medium, about 7 to 8 minutes (or more or less time for other degrees of doneness). Place a burger on top of each salad. Serve immediately.

*G*rilled Apple-and-Onion-Stuffed Quail Variation

½ cup whole hazelnuts	1 Granny Smith apple
1 tablespoon unsalted butter	4 whole quail, partially boned (see page 47)
½ cup finely minced onion	salt and freshly ground black pepper to taste
2 tablespoons dry sherry	

Preheat the oven to 325 degrees Fahrenheit.

Toast, skin, and process the hazelnuts as previously described for the dressing. Set aside until needed.

Heat the butter in a large nonstick sauté pan over medium heat. When hot, add the onion and cook until tender, about 10 minutes. Add the sherry wine and simmer for 5 minutes, until almost dry.

While the onions are simmering, peel, core, and finely chop the apple. Add the apple and ground hazelnuts to the onion mixture and continue to cook over medium heat, stirring occasionally, for 10 minutes. Remove from the heat and transfer to a 3-quart stainless steel bowl. Cool in an ice and water bath until thoroughly chilled. Cover the bowl with plastic wrap and refrigerate until needed.

Stuff the inside of each quail with about ¼ cup of the onion and apple mixture. At this point the quail can be individually wrapped in plastic wrap and refrigerated for up to 3 days.

Preheat the oven to 300 degrees Fahrenheit.

Season the quail with salt and pepper and grill over a medium wood or charcoal fire for 3 minutes on each side, until golden brown. Place the quail in the preheated oven and cook for 15 minutes, until thoroughly done but still juicy. Place a cooked quail on top of each salad. Serve immediately.

The Chef's Touch

OUR EVENING pantry supervisor at The Trellis, Gisele Hicks, suggested we discontinue the purchase of the hazelnut oil we loved so much for its distinctive flavor. During the fifteen years she has run the evening pantry (where we prepare salads, dressings, cold appetizers, et cetera), her strong French accent and fast-paced style of work have left many of our culinarians a bit bemused. But there was nothing confusing about the fact that we used quite a bit of very expensive hazelnut oil at The Trellis, and because hazelnut oil is very perishable, we were losing as much as we were using. So Gisele came up with the idea of infusing a virtually flavorless (and inexpensive) safflower vegetable oil with crushed hazelnuts. It works! The flavor is intense, the texture is enhancing, and the shelf life is significantly better than the expensive imported oil.

The Sherry Wine Dressing recipe yields about 1 cup. The dressing may be kept at room temperature for several hours before using or refrigerated in a covered, noncorrosive container for several days. If refrigerated, allow the dressing to return to room temperature and whisk vigorously before using.

The nuts for the dressing and the salad base (and the quail if you are using that variation) may all be toasted at the same time on the same baking sheet. If the nuts are not to be used on the day they are toasted, they may be stored in a sealed plastic container at room temperature for several days.

Any tart green apple may work with this recipe, but I highly recommend the Granny Smith variety. It has a crunch and flavor that never disappoints.

The Chef's Touch

Select your favorite regional sharp or medium-sharp cheddar cheese if your loyalties draw you away from the Empire State. I have been particularly fond of Oregon Tillamook cheddar ever since we used it to make our popular Cheddar Cheese Soup at The Trellis.

One large head of romaine lettuce, about 1½ pounds as purchased, should yield ¾ pound of prepared lettuce. For crisp greens, spin-dry the washed romaine lettuce pieces in a salad spinner.

Although the veal burger is certainly delicious with this salad, I admit that the quail is my favorite. You can serve the quail on the salad directly from the grill or cool the birds to room temperature, cover with plastic wrap, and hold at room temperature for 2 to 3 hours before serving. You should be able to locate quail at a specialty food store or upscale supermarket. Purchase birds that have been partially boned—that is, all the bones in the interior of the breast cavity have been removed (the leg and thigh bones remain).

A white French burgundy, preferably young and fruity, would play off the tartness of the apple and the richness of the hazelnuts.

Marinated Carrots and Leeks with Boston Lettuce, Scallion Fettuccine, and Rice Wine Vinaigrette

Serves 4

Scallion Fettuccine

$^{1}/_{2}$ cup finely chopped scallions, green part
   only
$^{1}/_{2}$ tablespoon peanut oil

$^{1}/_{2}$ teaspoon salt
2 cups all-purpose flour
2 large eggs

Rice Wine Vinaigrette

4 tablespoons rice wine vinegar
3 tablespoons soy sauce
2 tablespoons fresh lemon juice
1 tablespoon granulated sugar
1 tablespoon creamy peanut butter

1 teaspoon minced garlic
1 tablespoon sesame oil
1 cup peanut oil
$^{1}/_{2}$ cup safflower oil
salt and freshly ground black pepper to taste

Marinated Carrots and Leeks

2 tablespoons sesame seeds
1 pound carrots
1 pound leeks

Rice Wine Vinaigrette
salt and freshly ground black pepper to taste

Salad Greens and Garnish

1 pound Boston lettuce, cored, separated
   into leaves, washed, and dried

1 bunch scallions, cleaned, trimmed, and
   thinly sliced on the bias

৯

MAKE THE SCALLION FETTUCCINE DOUGH

Combine the scallions, peanut oil, and salt in the bowl of a food processor fitted with a metal blade. Process for 2 minutes, stopping to scrape down the bowl 2 or 3 times, until smooth.

Place 1¾ cups flour on a clean, dry work surface or in a 7-quart bowl. Make a well in the center of the flour large enough to hold the eggs and the scallion mixture. Using a fork, thoroughly combine the eggs and the scallion mixture, then gradually work the flour into this mixture, a small amount at a time. Once you've added enough flour so that you can handle the dough, begin kneading by hand. Knead until all the flour has been incorporated, about 10 minutes. Wrap the dough in plastic wrap and set aside at room temperature for 1 hour while you make the vinaigrette and marinated vegetables.

MAKE THE RICE WINE VINAIGRETTE

While the dough is relaxing, make the vinaigrette. In a 3-quart stainless steel bowl, whisk together the rice wine vinegar, soy sauce, lemon juice, sugar, peanut butter, and garlic. Slowly whisk in the sesame oil, followed by the peanut oil and safflower oil, maintaining a slow, steady stream until thoroughly incorporated. Season with salt and pepper. Cover with plastic wrap and set aside at room temperature until needed.

PREPARE THE MARINATED CARROTS AND LEEKS

Preheat the oven to 325 degrees Fahrenheit.

Toast the sesame seeds on a baking sheet in the preheated oven about 10 minutes, until light golden brown.

Peel and trim the ends from the carrots. Cut each carrot in half lengthwise, then cut each half diagonally into sticks 3 inches long, ½ inch wide, and ⅛ inch thick. Remove the green tops from the leeks, discarding the tops or saving them for flavoring a stock. Cut the leeks in half lengthwise, then rinse each half under cold running water while rubbing to re-

---

Equipment

cook's knife
cutting board
measuring cup
measuring spoons
vegetable peeler
paring knife
salad spinner
food processor with metal
  blade
rubber spatula
plastic wrap
3-quart stainless steel bowl
whisk
baking sheet
5-quart saucepan
colander
two 7-quart stainless steel
  bowls
pasta machine
tongs

Flounder variation requires:
pie tin
2 large nonstick sauté
  pans
spatula
paper towels

Chicken variation requires:
four 8- to 10-inch bamboo
  or metal skewers
charcoal grill

move any grit or dirt. Cut the leek halves into strips 3 inches long and ¼ inch wide. Blanch the carrots and leeks in 3 quarts of boiling salted water for 1½ to 2 minutes, until just slightly tender. Immediately transfer to ice water to stop the cooking.

Drain the carrots and leeks in a colander, then transfer to a 7-quart stainless steel bowl. Vigorously whisk the vinaigrette and add ⅔ cup to the carrots and leeks. (Cover the remaining 1⅓ cups of vinaigrette and set aside until needed.) Add the toasted sesame seeds and toss to combine. Season with salt and pepper. Cover with plastic wrap and set aside at room temperature until needed or refrigerate in a covered, noncorrosive container for up to 3 days.

CUT AND COOK THE FETTUCCINE

Cut the fettuccine dough into 4 equal pieces. Roll and knead each piece through the pasta machine, using the remaining ¼ cup of flour as necessary to prevent the dough from becoming sticky. Cut each sheet of dough into fettuccine.

Bring 3 quarts of salted water to a boil in a 5-quart saucepan over high heat. When boiling, add the fettuccine and cook, stirring frequently, until tender but slightly firm to the bite, about 1 minute. Drain the cooked fettuccine in a colander, then shake the colander to remove as much excess water from the fettuccine as possible. Transfer the well-drained fettuccine to a 7-quart stainless steel bowl. Vigorously whisk the vinaigrette and add ⅔ cup to the fettuccine. (Cover the remaining ⅔ cup of vinaigrette with plastic wrap and set aside until needed.) Season with salt and pepper and toss to coat the pasta with the vinaigrette. Cover loosely with plastic wrap and set aside for up to 1 hour before serving.

ASSEMBLE THE SALAD

Place equal amounts of scallion fettuccine in each of four 10- to 12-inch room-temperature soup or pasta plates. Create a well in the center of the pasta about 2½ inches in diameter. Divide and arrange the Boston lettuce leaves to form a cup inside the well of each fettuccine portion. Vigorously whisk the remaining ⅔ cup of vinaigrette and dress each portion of lettuce and fettuccine with 2 to 3 tablespoons of vinaigrette. Place an equal amount of marinated carrots and leeks inside each cup of Boston lettuce. Sprinkle sliced scallions over each salad and serve immediately.

§

*P*anfried Sesame Seed–Coated Flounder Fillet Variation

2 tablespoons sesame seeds

1 tablespoon fresh lemon juice

1 pound skinless flounder fillets, cut into strips 5 to 6 inches long and 1½ to 2 inches wide

salt and freshly ground black pepper to taste

1 cup all-purpose flour

½ cup peanut oil

Preheat the oven to 325 degrees Fahrenheit.

Toast the sesame seeds on an ungreased baking sheet in the preheated oven about 10 minutes, until light golden brown. Set aside to cool at room temperature.

Sprinkle the lemon juice over the flounder fillet strips. Lightly season with salt and pepper. Sprinkle the sesame seeds over both sides of the fillet strips, gently pressing them in to adhere. Place the flour in a pie tin or similar shallow dish. Place the strips in the flour one at a time and coat each side lightly but evenly. Transfer each strip to a baking sheet.

Heat ¼ cup of peanut oil in each of 2 large nonstick sauté pans over medium-high heat. When the oil is hot, divide the flounder strips into the 2 pans and panfry for 3 to 4 minutes on each side, until golden brown and crispy. Transfer the fillets to a baking sheet lined with paper towels. Allow the panfried flounder to stand for a minute or so, until any excess grease is absorbed by the paper. Arrange an equal amount of panfried flounder strips on each salad. Serve immediately or place the panfried flounder in a preheated 200-degree Fahrenheit oven to keep warm for up to 30 minutes.

§

*G*rilled Skewer of Ginger Chicken Variation

¼ cup soy sauce

1 tablespoon granulated sugar

½ tablespoon grated fresh ginger

½ teaspoon cayenne pepper

1½ pounds boneless, skinless chicken breasts, cut into 1-inch cubes

In a 3-quart stainless steel bowl, whisk together the soy sauce, sugar, ginger, and cayenne pepper. Add the chicken breast pieces and gently toss to combine. Cover tightly with plastic wrap and refrigerate for 1 hour.

Remove the chicken from the refrigerator and divide into 4 equal portions. Place each portion onto a skewer. Grill the skewers over a medium wood or charcoal fire for 10 minutes, turning frequently to brown evenly. (The chicken skewers may also be pan-seared in a large nonstick sauté pan over medium-high heat. Cook for about the same amount of time as listed for grilling.) Remove the chicken from the skewers and place each portion onto individual salads. Serve immediately or place the chicken skewers in a preheated 200-degree-Fahrenheit oven to keep warm for up to 20 minutes.

The Chef's Touch

FUSION COOKING, the melding of ingredients commonly associated with specific ethnic heritage, gained wide popularity in the 90s. Many ingredients customarily associated with a particular country have broad, if not worldwide, usage. Cilantro and Mexican cooking come to mind, but cilantro is endemic to several cuisines, including French (they usually refer to it as coriander), Italian, Chinese, and, of course, our own southwestern. Some may regard this salad as a "fusion" of Asian and American, but I prefer to say that all the flavors at play among the pasta, vinaigrette, vegetables, and greens come together on the plate and the palate for a delicious, rather than exotic, experience.

For advance preparation of the fettuccine, toss the cut fettuccine with ½ cup of cornmeal (to prevent the strands from sticking to each other during refrigeration), then place the pasta on a baking sheet lined with parchment paper. Cover tightly with plastic wrap and refrigerate up to 3 days, until ready to cook. Be sure to shake the cornmeal off the fettuccine before cooking it in boiling water.

The Rice Wine Vinaigrette recipe yields 2 cups. The vinaigrette may be kept at room temperature for several hours before using or refrigerated in a covered, noncorrosive container for 2 to 3 days. If refrigerated, return the vinaigrette to room temperature and whisk vigorously before using.

The Chef's Touch

One large head of Boston lettuce, about 1 pound as purchased, should yield the necessary ½ pound of prepared lettuce. For crisp greens, spin-dry the washed Boston lettuce leaves in a salad spinner.

For some delicious crunch, garnish this salad with toasted peanuts. Toast 1 cup of peanuts on a baking sheet in a preheated 325-degree-Fahrenheit oven for 10 to 12 minutes, until golden brown. Cool the nuts to room temperature before sprinkling an equal amount on each salad.

The Alsace region of France produces some extraordinary wines, such as Riesling and gewürztraminer, that are, sadly, not well known or routinely consumed here in the United States. Many American consumers associate those wines with Germany rather than France. The Alsatian versions are markedly drier than their German counterparts. A recent-vintage, vibrantly spicy gewürztraminer from the Alsatian wine shipper Trimbach would be particularly appealing with this salad.

Spicy Garden Slaw with Leaf Lettuce, Toasted Peanuts, Crispy Corn Biscuits, and Cayenne Dressing

4 servings

Cayenne Dressing

3 tablespoons cider vinegar
2 tablespoons fresh lemon juice
2 teaspoons Dijon-style mustard
1 teaspoon hot sauce

½ teaspoon ground cayenne pepper
½ teaspoon celery seeds
1 cup safflower oil
salt and freshly ground black pepper to taste

Spicy Garden Slaw

½ small head green cabbage (about ¾ to 1 pound), outer leaves removed, washed, cored, quartered, and thinly sliced
½ small head red cabbage (about ¾ to 1 pound), outer leaves removed, washed, cored, quartered, and thinly sliced
¼ pound carrots, peeled, ends trimmed, and cut lengthwise into sticks 3 inches long and ¼ inch thick
1 medium red onion (about 6 ounces), peeled and thinly sliced
1 medium green bell pepper (about 6 ounces), washed, cut in half lengthwise, core removed, seeded, membrane removed, and cut into thin strips the length of the pepper

1 medium red bell pepper (about 6 ounces), washed, cut in half lengthwise, core removed, seeded, membrane removed, and cut into thin strips the length of the pepper
1 medium yellow bell pepper (about 6 ounces), washed, cut in half lengthwise, core removed, seeded, membrane removed, and cut into thin strips the length of the pepper
¾ cup Cayenne Dressing
1 cup unsalted Virginia peanuts

Crispy Corn Biscuits

1 cup all-purpose flour
$^1/_2$ cup yellow cornmeal
$^1/_4$ teaspoon baking soda
1 teaspoon baking powder

$^1/_2$ teaspoon salt
4 tablespoons vegetable shortening
$^1/_2$ cup cooked corn, well drained
$^1/_4$ cup buttermilk

Salad Greens

$^3/_4$ pound red leaf lettuce, cored, separated
   into leaves, washed, and dried

Equipment
measuring spoons
measuring cup
cook's knife
cutting board
vegetable peeler
paring knife
salad spinner
7-quart stainless steel bowl
whisk
1-quart stainless steel bowl
plastic wrap
rubber spatula
2 baking sheets
(1 nonstick)
electric mixer with paddle
rolling pin
2½-inch round biscuit
cutter
Chicken leg variation
* requires:*
baking dish with cover
charcoal grill
tongs
basting brush
Smoked catfish variation
* requires:*
3-quart stainless steel bowl
paper towels
smoker
spatula

MAKE THE CAYENNE DRESSING
In a 7-quart stainless steel bowl, whisk together the cider vinegar, lemon juice, mustard, hot sauce, cayenne pepper, and celery seeds. Add the safflower oil in a slow, steady stream while whisking to incorporate. Season with salt and pepper, and whisk to combine. Transfer $^3/_4$ cup of the dressing to a 1-quart stainless steel bowl, cover tightly with plastic wrap, and set aside until needed. Leave the remaining $^3/_4$ cup uncovered in the 7-quart bowl.

PREPARE THE SPICY GARDEN SLAW
Preheat the oven to 325 degrees Fahrenheit.
Add the prepared green and red cabbages, carrots, red onion, green, red, and yellow bell peppers to the dressing in the 7-quart bowl. Toss to combine thoroughly. Cover tightly with plastic wrap and refrigerate until ready to serve. (The slaw may be kept refrigerated in a covered, noncorrosive container for up to 2 days before serving.)
Toast the peanuts on a baking sheet in the preheated oven for 10 to 12 minutes, until golden brown. Set the nuts aside at room temperature until needed.

MAKE THE BISCUITS
Preheat the oven to 400 degrees Fahrenheit.
Place the flour, cornmeal, baking soda, baking powder, and

salt in the bowl of an electric mixer fitted with a paddle. Mix on low speed until thoroughly combined, about 30 seconds. Add the shortening and mix on low speed for 1 minute, until the shortening is "cut into" the flour mixture and resembles coarse meal. Add the corn and buttermilk, then mix on low speed until the dough begins to come together, about 30 seconds. Transfer the dough to a clean, dry, lightly floured work surface.

Roll the dough out ½ inch thick. (If the dough sticks to the rolling pin or work surface, use a small amount of extra flour to prevent sticking.) Cut the dough into 8 biscuits using a 2½-inch biscuit cutter. Form the remaining dough into a ball and roll it out again to a thickness of ½ inch. Cut the dough into 4 biscuits. Transfer the biscuits to a nonstick baking sheet. Bake the biscuits on the center rack of the preheated oven for 12 minutes, rotating the baking sheet 180 degrees about halfway through the baking time, until very lightly golden brown. Remove the biscuits from the oven and set aside at room temperature while assembling the salad.

ASSEMBLE THE SALAD
Divide and arrange the red leaf lettuce leaves on four 10- to 12-inch room-temperature plates.

Whisk the dressing in the 1-quart bowl. Dress the red leaf lettuce on each plate with 2 to 3 tablespoons of dressing. Place an equal amount of spicy garden slaw on the center of each salad.

Sprinkle toasted peanuts on each portion of spicy garden slaw. Serve immediately accompanied by the crispy corn biscuits.

§

*B*arbecued Chicken Leg Variation

1 tablespoon dry mustard
1 tablespoon salt
1 teaspoon ground celery seeds
½ teaspoon cayenne pepper
½ teaspoon white pepper

4 chicken leg and thigh portions
1 cup dark beer
1 cup Trellis Barbecue Sauce (see page 24)
  or your own favorite

Preheat the oven to 300 degrees Fahrenheit.
Combine the dry mustard, salt, celery seeds, cayenne pepper, and white pepper.

Place the chicken in a baking dish. Sprinkle the dry seasoning mixture over the chicken, coating all sides. Pour the beer into the baking dish, then cover with a lid or aluminum foil. Place the baking dish in the preheated oven and cook the chicken for 45 minutes. Remove the dish from the oven and transfer the chicken to a clean dish. The chicken can be grilled immediately or cooled to room temperature, covered with plastic wrap, and refrigerated for up to 24 hours before grilling.

Before grilling, lightly coat the chicken legs with about ⅓ the amount of barbecue sauce. Grill the legs over a medium-low wood or charcoal fire for 5 to 7 minutes, turning as necessary to prevent overcharring. Baste the legs with the remaining barbecue sauce while continuing to cook and turn the legs for 5 to 7 more minutes. Remove the legs from the grill. Place a leg onto each salad. Serve immediately. (The chicken legs may also be kept warm in a preheated 200-degree-Fahrenheit oven for up to 30 minutes.)

Smoked Catfish Fillet Variation

½ cup warm water
¼ cup soy sauce
2 tablespoons granulated sugar

½ cup cool water
4 5- to 6-ounce skinless farm-raised catfish fillets

Prepare the brine in a 3-quart stainless steel bowl by combining the warm water, soy sauce, and sugar. Whisk to dissolve the sugar. Add the cool water and stir to combine. Immerse the catfish in the brine for 1 minute. Transfer the catfish to a baking sheet lined with paper towels to drain for 1 to 2 minutes.

Line the top shelf of a smoker with parchment paper. Place the catfish fillets on the shelf in the smoker and smoke for 1 hour. If you lack a smoker, the catfish can be grilled. Basting with barbecue sauce would be a nice touch.

Preheat the oven to 325 degrees Fahrenheit.

Remove the catfish from the smoker and transfer to a nonstick baking sheet. Place the catfish in the preheated oven for 8 minutes. Remove the catfish fillets from the oven, transfer to a cool baking sheet, then refrigerate until the fillets are thoroughly chilled, about 1 hour. Place a fillet on each salad. Serve immediately.

COLESLAW IS beloved by many, with variations as plentiful as there are cooks: a little celery seed here, some caraway seed there . . . cabbage cut thin, or should it be coarse? . . . mayonnaise dressing versus vinaigrette . . . a tender cabbage like savoy or the most pungent one you can find? . . . a sprinkling of chopped bacon or julienne apple slices, or both? I think you have the picture. I hope you will enjoy this rendition, with its piquant and fiery dressing highlighting a medley of fresh vegetables, and the added crunch of toasted peanuts. It may not be what Mom used to make, but it's sure to please.

The spicy Cayenne Dressing recipe yields about 1½ cups. The dressing may be kept at room temperature for several hours before using or refrigerated in a covered, noncorrosive container for 2 to 3 days. If refrigerated, return the dressing to room temperature and whisk vigorously before using.

Each ½ head of cabbage yields 4 cups of sliced cabbage. And by the way, I subscribe to the "never too thin" school when it comes to cutting cabbage for coleslaw.

Our Crispy Corn Biscuits are a bit odd as biscuits go. They are thin but light, and not fluffy at all; in some ways they are more like a cracker than a biscuit.

I hope you can purchase fresh farm-raised catfish in your neck of the woods. I prefer the farm-raised, although for years we served local channel catfish at The Trellis. (We switched to farm-raised due to the erratic supply of the channel catfish.) The sweet, tender, and white *fresh* farm-raised catfish is revelatory to some of our guests who have only encountered mud-hugging catfish that absorb their murky surroundings in flavor, color, and texture.

One medium head of red leaf lettuce, about ¾ pound as purchased, should yield ½ pound of prepared leaves. For crisp greens, spin-dry the red leaf lettuce leaves in a salad spinner.

A frosty cold bottle of beer would be my beverage preference with this salad. With all the excellent regional microbrews currently available, I will leave the specific selection up to you.

Baby Salad Greens and Sliced Tomatoes with Asiago Cheese, Toasted Pine Nuts, Herbed Olive Flat Bread, and Basil Vinaigrette

Serves 4

Herbed Olive Flat Bread

2 teaspoons granulated sugar

1¼ cups warm water

1 tablespoon active dry yeast

2½ cups all-purpose flour

¾ cup yellow cornmeal

40 Mediterranean olives, pitted and chopped

10 tablespoons extra-virgin olive oil

2 tablespoons chopped fresh basil

1 tablespoon chopped fresh Italian parsley

1 teaspoon salt

1 teaspoon kosher salt

Basil Vinaigrette

¾ cup extra-virgin olive oil

4 tablespoons red wine vinegar

2 tablespoons chopped fresh basil leaves

salt and freshly ground black pepper to taste

Salad Greens and Garnish

½ cup pine nuts

4 medium tomatoes (about 1½ pounds), washed, cored, and sliced ¼ inch thick

2 tablespoons freshly cracked black peppercorns

kosher salt to taste

½ pound trimmed, washed, and dried baby salad greens

¼ pound Wisconsin Asiago cheese, shaved with a cheese shaver or vegetable peeler

Equipment

measuring spoons
measuring cup
cook's knife
cutting board
paring knife
salad spinner
cheese shaver or vegetable
    peeler
table-model electric mixer
    with dough hook
rubber spatula
plastic wrap
10- by 15-inch baking
    sheet with sides
parchment paper
pastry brush
3-quart stainless steel bowl
whisk
baking sheet

Duck variation requires:
aluminum foil
meat cleaver
large nonstick sauté pan
tongs
sharp slicer

Salmon variation requires:
slotted spatula
paper towels

PREPARE THE HERBED OLIVE FLAT BREAD

In the bowl of an electric mixer, dissolve the sugar in ½ cup of warm water. Add the yeast and stir to dissolve. Set the bowl aside, uncovered, for 5 minutes, so the yeast can foam and come to life.

Add the flour, cornmeal, olives, 6 tablespoons of olive oil, basil, parsley, salt, and the remaining ¾ cup of warm water. Using the dough hook of the mixer, combine the ingredients on medium speed for 2 minutes. Stop the mixer and scrape down the sides of the bowl. Mix on low speed until the dough is smooth and elastic, about 5 to 6 minutes.

Remove the bowl from the mixer. Drizzle 1 tablespoon of olive oil over the dough in the bowl and turn the dough several times to coat with oil. Cover the bowl with plastic wrap and place in a warm location so the dough can rise until doubled in volume, about 45 to 50 minutes.

Preheat the oven to 400 degrees Fahrenheit.

Lightly coat a 10- by 15-inch baking sheet with sides with ½ tablespoon olive oil. Line the oiled baking sheet with parchment paper, then lightly coat the paper with an additional ½ tablespoon of olive oil. Place the dough on the baking sheet and flatten by hand into a rectangle measuring approximately 9 by 13 inches. Brush the top of the dough with the remaining 2 tablespoons of olive oil. Sprinkle the kosher salt evenly over the dough.

Bake in the preheated oven about 18 to 20 minutes, until lightly browned. Remove the flat bread from the oven and cool to room temperature before cutting into desired pieces.

MAKE THE BASIL VINAIGRETTE

In a 3-quart stainless steel bowl, vigorously whisk together the olive oil, red wine vinegar, and basil. Season with salt and pepper. Cover with plastic wrap and set aside at room temperature until needed.

FINISH AND ASSEMBLE THE SALAD

Preheat the oven to 325 degrees Fahrenheit.

Toast the pine nuts in the preheated oven for 10 minutes, until golden brown. Cool to room temperature before using.

Place the tomato slices on a baking sheet or large platter covered with plastic wrap. Sprinkle both sides of the tomato slices with the peppercorns and kosher salt.

Divide and arrange the tomato slices on four 10- to 12-inch room-temperature plates. Arrange an equal amount of greens in a mound in the center of the tomato slices. Vigorously whisk the vinaigrette. Dress the tomatoes and greens on each plate with 3 to 4 tablespoons of vinaigrette. Place an equal amount of Wisconsin Asiago cheese on the greens on each plate. Sprinkle the toasted pine nuts over each salad. Serve immediately accompanied by the herbed olive flat bread.

❧

*H*oney-Charred Duck Breast Variation

4 3- to 4-ounce boneless, skinless duck breasts, trimmed of excess fat and membrane

salt to taste

¼ cup plus 1 teaspoon extra-virgin olive oil

2 tablespoons balsamic vinegar

2 tablespoons honey

1 tablespoon freshly cracked black peppercorns

Preheat the oven to 350 degrees Fahrenheit.

Place the duck breasts, one at a time, between 2 sheets of lightly oiled aluminum foil or parchment paper. Slightly flatten each breast using a meat cleaver or the bottom of a heavy-duty sauté pan. Lightly season both sides of each duck breast with salt.

In a 3-quart stainless steel bowl, whisk together ¼ cup of olive oil, balsamic vinegar, honey, and peppercorns. Whisk to combine. Place the duck breasts in the marinade and stir to coat.

Heat a large nonstick sauté pan over high heat. When the pan is smoking hot, remove the duck breasts from the marinade and place in the pan. Char the breasts for 1 minute on each side. Remove the breasts from the pan and transfer to a nonstick baking sheet. Place the baking sheet in the preheated oven and cook the breasts for 10 minutes (this will yield deliciously tender medium-rare duck; cook longer for less tender and more well-done duck). Transfer the breasts to a cutting board and use a sharp slicer to slice each breast into thin slices at a slight angle across the grain. Arrange the duck meat on the salads in a fan. Serve immediately.

$

*H*erb-Roasted Salmon Steak Variation

4 5-ounce skinless salmon steaks
salt and freshly ground black pepper to taste
2 tablespoons extra-virgin olive oil

3 tablespoons chopped fresh Italian parsley
2 tablespoons chopped fresh chives
1 tablespoon chopped fresh basil

Preheat the oven to 375 degrees Fahrenheit.

Place the salmon steaks on a 10- or 12-inch plate. Season both sides of the salmon steaks with salt and pepper. Drizzle the olive oil over the steaks, turning them to coat both sides.

Combine the parsley, chives, and basil on a separate plate. Roll each salmon steak, one at a time, in the herb mixture to coat all sides evenly and thoroughly. Place the salmon steaks on a nonstick baking sheet with sides. Place the baking sheet in the preheated oven and roast the salmon for 12 to 14 minutes for medium rare or longer for more well-done fish.

Remove the fish from the oven and use a slotted spatula to transfer them to a baking sheet lined with paper towels to drain for a few seconds. Place the salmon steaks on the salads. Serve immediately.

The Chef's Touch

ALTHOUGH ITALIAN flat bread is not a quick bread (bread leavened without yeast), it is nevertheless quick to make. Perhaps that is one reason that flat bread, or focaccia, is becoming ubiquitous in restaurants these days. Another reason for its omnipresence is the popularity of Mediterranean cuisine, a trend I fully support. While flat bread is not included in our bread basket at The Trellis, you will find it in sandwiches (my favorite is the sweet potato flat bread used with a vegetarian sandwich at lunch) and sliced in half and grilled to accompany certain Trellis dinner specials.

The Basil Vinaigrette recipe yields 1 cup. The vinaigrette may be kept at room temperature for several hours before using or refrigerated in a covered, noncorrosive container for 2 to 3 days. If refrigerated, return the vinaigrette to room temperature and whisk vigorously before using.

Talk about ubiquitous, fresh basil is practically available year-round! My only quibble is its short shelf life. Fresh leaves, especially those with the root ends snipped off, are delicate and usually stay bright green for only 2 to 3 days in the refrigerator. My advice is to purchase only what is needed for a particular recipe. Can you substitute dried basil for this recipe? Don't you dare!

This salad may suggest summer more than other seasons, but it's not out of the question to consider serving it any time of the year, even in January (when we tested the recipe for this book). So what to do about the tasteless tomatoes found during many months of the year? First try locating "on the vine" tomatoes from Spain. These tomatoes are finding their way into many fresh market grocery stores, and they are quite good. Beautifully colored, nicely textured, and offering obvious fruit flavor, they are a bit pricey but worth trying. Look for vine clusters with 4 to 5 tomatoes. When you fail to find naturally good-flavored tomatoes, try marinating the tomato slices in some basil vinaigrette (make additional for this purpose). After slicing and seasoning the tomatoes, spoon vinaigrette over the slices and set them aside at room temperature for an hour or so before serving.

Why use kosher salt? I like the tactile quality of the coarse grain, and it's additive-free. But note that it has half the intensity of refined table salt, so when you sprinkle it on the tomatoes, be generous. How generous? Visualize pretzels.

All sorts of young salad greens are making their way to the market. Sorrel, spinach, Swiss chard, Boston lettuce, limestone lettuce, arugula, dandelion, and many more are being sold at their tenderest moment. They are indeed delicious when so young and additionally lend themselves to being served as a mixture. Purchase good-quality baby greens that require very little trimming. For crisp young salad greens, spin-dry the washed greens in a salad spinner.

For this recipe we used Wisconsin Asiago cheese, a semi-hard cheese produced from cow's milk that is a delicious alternative to Parmesan. You may also purchase Italian Asiago, the Italian forebear to the Wisconsin version. Whatever you decide, select a young, semi-hard cheese for this recipe rather than a mature, hard, and granular cheese.

A *slightly* chilled youthful Beaujolais-Villages, bursting with succulent fruit, creates a sense of well-being when enjoyed with this salad—even on a winter day when tomatoes are not in season.

Beans

*P*an-Seared Yukon Gold Potatoes with Green Beans, Jicama, Red Onion Relish, and Parsley Dressing

Serves 4

Red Onion Relish

¼ cup extra-virgin olive oil
3 large red onions (about 1½ pounds),
   peeled and thinly sliced
salt and freshly ground black pepper to taste

1 tablespoon granulated sugar
¾ cup dried cranberries
¼ cup raspberry vinegar

Parsley Dressing

2 tablespoons white wine vinegar
1 tablespoon fresh lemon juice
1 tablespoon Dijon-style mustard

½ cup extra-virgin olive oil
2 tablespoons chopped fresh Italian parsley
salt and freshly ground black pepper to taste

Green Beans

1 pound tiny green beans or slender bright-
   green snap beans, trimmed

Yukon Gold Potatoes

4 medium Yukon Gold potatoes (about
  2 pounds), washed

2 tablespoons extra-virgin olive oil
salt and freshly ground black pepper to taste

Salad Greens and Garnish

1 cup sliced almonds
1 pound Boston lettuce, cored, separated
  into leaves, washed, and dried

½ pound jicama, peeled and cut into strips
  3 inches long and ¼ inch thick

Equipment

measuring cup
paring knife
cook's knife
cutting board
measuring spoons
lettuce spinner
5-quart saucepan
kitchen spoon
2-quart noncorrosive
    container
3-quart stainless steel bowl
whisk
plastic wrap
colander
baking sheet
basting brush
2 large nonstick sauté
    pans
spatula
nonstick baking sheet

*Red snapper variation
    requires:*
7½- by 12-inch shallow
    glass baking dish
1½-quart saucepan
aluminum foil
slotted spatula
paper towels

Chicken variation requires:
aluminum foil
meat cleaver
tongs

❧

PREPARE THE RED ONION RELISH

Heat the olive oil in a 5-quart saucepan over medium heat. When the oil is hot, add the onions and season with salt and pepper. Cook, stirring often, until tender, about 15 minutes. Remove the saucepan from the heat. Add the sugar and stir to dissolve. Add the cranberries and raspberry vinegar, and stir to combine. Transfer the relish to a 2-quart noncorrosive container and cool to room temperature, then cover and refrigerate for at least 24 hours before serving.

MAKE THE PARSLEY DRESSING

In a 3-quart stainless steel bowl, whisk together the white wine vinegar, lemon juice, and mustard. Add the olive oil in a slow, steady stream while whisking until incorporated. Add the parsley, salt, and pepper, and whisk to combine. Cover with plastic wrap and hold at room temperature until needed.

COOK THE GREEN BEANS

Heat 3 quarts of salted water in a 5-quart saucepan over medium-high heat. When the water boils, add the green beans and cook until tender, about 4 to 6 minutes, depending on the thickness of the bean. Drain the beans in a colander, then immediately plunge into ice water to stop the cooking and keep the beans bright green. Remove from the ice water and drain thoroughly. Cover with plastic wrap and refrigerate until needed.

PREPARE THE YUKON GOLD POTATOES

Preheat the oven to 400 degrees Fahrenheit.

Pierce each potato 2 or 3 times with a fork. Bake the potatoes on a baking sheet in the preheated oven for 50 minutes, until cooked through. Transfer the potatoes to a large dish and place, uncovered, in the refrigerator for about 1 hour or so, until thoroughly cooled.

Preheat the oven to 225 degrees Fahrenheit.

Slice the potatoes into ¼-inch-thick slices. The sliced potatoes may be covered with plastic wrap and refrigerated for up to 2 days before pan-searing. Lightly brush the potato slices with the olive oil. Generously season both sides of the potato slices with salt and pepper. Heat 2 large nonstick sauté pans over medium-high heat. When the pans are hot, add the potato slices and cook for 4 to 5 minutes on each side, until golden brown. Transfer the potato slices to a nonstick baking sheet. Keep the potato slices in the preheated oven until ready to serve, up to 30 minutes.

FINISH AND ASSEMBLE THE SALAD

Preheat the oven to 325 degrees Fahrenheit.

Toast the sliced almonds on a baking sheet in the preheated oven about 14 minutes, until golden brown. Set aside to cool at room temperature.

Divide and arrange the Boston lettuce leaves on four 10- to 12-inch room-temperature plates. Combine the green beans with the jicama strips. Place an equal amount of beans and jicama in the center of each bed of lettuce. Vigorously whisk the parsley dressing. Dress the beans, jicama, and lettuce with 2 to 3 tablespoons of dressing. Arrange 4 to 6 slices of the Yukon Gold potato slices around each portion of beans and jicama. Spoon 3 to 4 tablespoons of red onion relish on the center of each salad. Sprinkle sliced almonds on each salad to garnish. Serve immediately.

Vinegar-Steamed Red Snapper Fillet Variation

4 4- to 5-ounce red snapper fillets
salt and freshly ground black pepper to taste
4 tablespoons roughly chopped Italian
    parsley
1 medium red onion (about 6 ounces),
    peeled and sliced into 12 slices ⅛ inch
    thick

¼ cup white wine vinegar
2 tablespoons extra-virgin olive oil

Preheat the oven to 375 degrees Fahrenheit.

Place the snapper fillets in a shallow glass baking dish, skin side down. Season with salt and pepper, then sprinkle 1 tablespoon of chopped parsley over each fillet. Cover each portion with 3 slices of red onion.

In a 1½-quart saucepan, whisk together the white wine vinegar and olive oil. Heat the mixture to a boil over high heat, then pour over the snapper fillets. Cover the baking dish tightly with aluminum foil. Place the dish in the preheated oven and bake the fish for 20 to 25 minutes, until cooked. Remove from the oven and use a slotted spatula to transfer the snapper fillets to a baking sheet lined with paper towels to drain for a few seconds. Place a snapper fillet on each salad. Serve immediately.

❧

*A*lmond-Crusted Sautéed Chicken Breast Variation

4 4-ounce boneless, skinless chicken breasts, trimmed of excess fat
2 tablespoons fresh lemon juice
2 tablespoons sauvignon blanc or other dry white wine

salt and freshly ground black pepper to taste
2 tablespoons plus 1 teaspoon extra-virgin olive oil
1 cup sliced almonds

Place the chicken breasts on a large platter or baking sheet with sides. Sprinkle both sides of the breasts with the lemon juice and white wine, and season each side with salt and pepper.

Place the breasts, one at a time, between two sheets of lightly oiled aluminum foil or parchment paper. Uniformly flatten each breast with a meat cleaver or the bottom of a heavy-duty sauté pan.

Crush the almonds into ⅛- to ¼-inch pieces. Coat both sides of each chicken breast with the crushed almonds, gently pressing them into the chicken so that they adhere.

Heat 1 tablespoon of olive oil in each of 2 large nonstick sauté pans over medium-high heat, or do one pan at a time. When the oil is hot, place 2 chicken breasts in each pan and sauté for 4 minutes, until golden brown. Turn the breasts and continue to cook for an additional 3 minutes. Remove the breasts from the pan and transfer them to a baking sheet lined with paper towels to drain for a few seconds. Place a chicken breast on each salad. Serve immediately.

The Chef's Touch

T H E   T R E L L I S has served salads with contrasting colors, alternating textures, and warm over cool temperatures for almost two decades. Typically, the list of ingredients itself looks like a rainbow, and in this salad the warm potatoes are the pot of gold bringing out all the flavors of the cool components.

The Red Onion Relish, which will keep refrigerated up to 2 weeks, is also a handsome and delicious accompaniment to sandwiches (especially turkey). Doubling or even quadrupling this recipe will merely extend the delicious outcome exponentially, without affecting the flavor.

The Parsley Dressing recipe yields ¾ cup. This dressing is best at room temperature and will keep for 2 to 3 hours; otherwise, you can refrigerate it in a covered, noncorrosive container for 2 to 3 days, but be sure to bring it to room temperature and whisk vigorously before using.

Yukon Gold potatoes were introduced to the American public with a bushel of marketing hoopla a few years ago. Touted as having a remarkably buttery flavor, they happily lived up to the advertising claims and quickly established themselves as a delicious, if pricey, option to more prosaic spuds. Look for firm, evenly colored potatoes and avoid wrinkled, cracked, and green-tinged specimens. Yukon Gold potatoes are more temperature sensitive than other tubers and are best stored at an air-conditioned room temperature. If too warm, they sprout and shrivel; too cold, they concentrate their sugars and taste awful.

What's *de rigueur* for green beans has changed as often as hemlines. For years they suffered from being overcooked until limp and tasting a lot like the fatback that shared the pot. Then came the *nouvelle* fashion, which left them undercooked, hard, and tasteless. Today, I recommend that you cook them until *just right*. The best way to do this is to taste a single bean every 15 seconds or so after the first 3 to 4 minutes of cooking, then remove the beans from the heat when the perceptible raw taste is gone. The beans will be tender, slightly crisp, and brilliantly green.

Jicama is available in most supermarkets virtually year-round now. This root vegetable looks a bit like a rutabaga, but that's where the similarities stop. The white flesh of the jicama has a sweet, almost nutty flavor and crisp texture when raw. The weight of a jicama is an indication of the quality. A root about 3

(*continued on next page*)

The Chef's Touch

to 3¼ inches in diameter should weigh around 9 to 10 ounces; if it weighs less, the center will probably be spongy.

One large head of Boston lettuce, about 1 pound as purchased, should yield ½ pound prepared lettuce. For crisp greens, spin-dry the washed Boston lettuce leaves in a salad spinner.

My friend and collaborator Nancy Thomas (Nancy illustrated *An Alphabet of Sweets*) stopped by Ganache Hill to say hello the day we were testing the recipe for this salad, and stayed to join us for lunch. Since we were not expecting her, we did not have a great "guest" wine to serve, but we did have a jug of Corbett Canyon California Sauvignon Blanc that was used for the Almond-Crusted Sautéed Chicken Breast variation, and since I never cook with wine that I would not drink, we gave it a try. It was not only very drinkable but had a sparkling floral character that complemented the expressively sweet flavors in the salad.

White Bean Salad with Crispy Leeks, Arugula, Spinach, and Rosemary Vinaigrette

4 servings

Rosemary Vinaigrette

6 tablespoons cider vinegar
2 tablespoons Dijon-style mustard
1/2 teaspoon finely minced fresh rosemary

1 cup extra-virgin olive oil
salt and freshly ground black pepper to taste

White Bean Salad

1 cup dried white beans, washed, picked over, and soaked for 12 hours in 1 quart cold water
1 tablespoon salt
1 pound red bliss potatoes, unpeeled, washed, cut into 1/4-inch cubes, and covered with cold water

2 medium tomatoes (about 3/4 pound), peeled, seeded, and chopped into 1/4-inch pieces
1 bunch scallions, thinly sliced on the diagonal
Rosemary Vinaigrette
freshly ground black pepper to taste

Crispy Leeks

1 1/2 pounds leeks

6 cups vegetable oil

Salad Greens

1/4 pound stemmed, washed, and dried arugula

1/4 pound stemmed, washed, and dried curly spinach

Equipment

measuring spoons
cook's knife
cutting board
measuring cup
colander
two 2-quart plastic
    containers
paring knife
5-quart saucepan
salad spinner
3-quart stainless steel bowl
whisk
plastic wrap
two 7-quart bowls
3-quart saucepan
rubber spatula
deep fryer with fry basket
    or heavy-gauge 4-quart
    saucepan with skimmer
candy/deep-frying
    thermometer
baking sheet
paper towels
slotted kitchen spoon

Duck variation requires:
5-quart stainless steel bowl
baking sheet with sides
wire rack

Cod variation requires:
large nonstick sauté pan
parchment paper
slotted spatula

МAKE THE ROSEMARY VINAIGRETTE

In a 3-quart stainless steel bowl, whisk together the cider vinegar, mustard, and rosemary. Add the olive oil in a slow, steady stream while whisking, until incorporated. Season with salt and pepper and whisk to combine. Cover with plastic wrap and set aside at room temperature until needed.

PREPARE THE WHITE BEAN SALAD

Drain the soaked beans in a colander. Rinse the beans with cold water and drain thoroughly before cooking.

Bring 2 quarts of water and 1 tablespoon of salt to a boil in a 5-quart saucepan over high heat. When the water boils, add the beans. Adjust the heat and simmer the beans about 30 minutes, until very tender. Drain the beans in a colander, then transfer to a 7-quart stainless steel bowl. Set aside while cooking the potatoes.

Bring 1 quart of lightly salted water to a boil in a 3-quart saucepan. Drain the cubed potatoes in a colander. When the water boils, add the potatoes. Adjust the heat and simmer the potatoes about 9 to 10 minutes, until cooked through. Drain the hot water from the potatoes, then cool the potatoes in the saucepan under cold running water. Thoroughly drain the potatoes in a colander. Add the cooked potatoes, tomatoes, and scallions to the bowl containing the white beans. Vigorously whisk the vinaigrette, then add ³⁄₄ cup to the bean mixture. Cover the remaining ¹⁄₂ cup with plastic wrap and set aside at room temperature until needed. Use a rubber spatula to stir the ingredients until combined. Season with salt and pepper. Cover the bowl with plastic wrap and set aside for up to 2 hours at room temperature. Or cool to room temperature and then refrigerate in a covered, noncorrosive container for up to 2 days before serving.

PREPARE THE LEEKS

Preheat the oven to 225 degrees Fahrenheit.

Remove the green tops and root end from the leeks, discarding the tops or saving them for flavoring a stock. Cut the leeks in half lengthwise, then rinse each half under cold running water to remove any grit or dirt. Cut the leek halves into strips 3 inches long and ⅛ inch wide.

Heat the vegetable oil in a deep fryer (or high-sided heavy-duty pot) fitted with a deep-frying basket over medium-high heat to a temperature of 325 degrees Fahrenheit.

Fry half of the leeks at a time for about 3½ minutes, until they attain a golden straw color. (At this point the leeks will not be crispy. This happens in the oven.) Transfer the leeks to a baking sheet lined with paper towels and hold in the preheated oven for 30 minutes, until crispy. (The leeks will stay crispy for an additional 15 to 20 minutes in the oven; lower the temperature to 200 degrees Fahrenheit.)

FINISH AND ASSEMBLE THE SALAD

Combine the arugula and spinach in a 7-quart stainless steel bowl. Vigorously whisk the remaining ½ cup of rosemary vinaigrette. Add to the greens and toss until the leaves are coated with the vinaigrette. (It may seem that the volume of vinaigrette is not sufficient to do this, but it is.) Divide and arrange the greens on four 10- to 12-inch room-temperature plates. Use a slotted spoon to place an equal amount of the white bean salad on the center of each portion of greens. Top each salad with fried leeks. Serve immediately.

❧

Roasted Cured Duck Leg Variation

3 tablespoons kosher salt	½ teaspoon chopped fresh rosemary
1½ tablespoons granulated sugar	¼ teaspoon minced garlic
¾ teaspoon chopped fresh thyme	4 duck leg and thigh portions

In a small dish, combine the kosher salt, sugar, thyme, rosemary, and garlic. Place the duck leg portions in a 5-quart stainless steel bowl. Sprinkle the mixture over the duck legs, covering as much surface area as possible. Cover the bowl with plastic wrap and refrigerate for 24 hours.

Preheat the oven to 325 degrees Fahrenheit.

Place the duck legs on a wire rack on a baking sheet with sides. Roast in the preheated oven for 1 hour, until crispy and browned. Transfer the duck legs to paper towels and cool to room temperature. When the duck legs are cool, use a sharp knife to trim as much meat away from the bones as possible. Cut the duck meat into thin strips. Place an equal amount of duck meat on the top of each salad. Serve immediately.

⅄

Lemon-Steamed Cod Fillet Variation

4 5- to 6-ounce skinless cod fillets
salt and freshly ground black pepper to taste
½ cup sauvignon blanc or other dry white
   wine

¼ cup water
2 tablespoons fresh lemon juice
1 teaspoon thinly sliced lemon zest
1 teaspoon chopped fresh rosemary

Season both sides of the cod fillets with salt and pepper.

Heat the wine, water, lemon juice, lemon zest, and fresh rosemary in a large nonstick sauté pan over medium-high heat. When the liquid begins to simmer, place the fillets, evenly spaced, in the pan. Cover the fish with a piece of parchment paper cut to fit the inside of the pan. Steam the fillets for 3½ minutes before turning. Steam for an additional 3½ to 4 minutes, until cooked through. Use a slotted spatula to transfer the fillets to a baking sheet lined with paper towels to drain for a few seconds. Place a cod fillet on each salad. Serve immediately.

The Chef's Touch

M Y   W I F E ,   Connie, and I spent several blissful weeks traveling in New Zealand a few years ago, thanks to an invitation to participate in a week-long soft-shell crab event at a friend's restaurant in Auckland. It was the perfect combination of vacation and work. The pristine beauty and drama of New Zealand's landscape will awe the most jaded traveler, and those New Zealanders certainly know how to eat, drink, and be merry.

I had met my restaurateur/friend Tony Adcock in 1985 in Florence, Italy, at a professional cooking course we took with Giuliano Bugialli. We became instant friends, over a glass or two of grappa, if I recall, and promised to do a culinary exchange at each other's restaurant. Tony came through for me in 1990. The night we arrived, we ate at Tony's restaurant, The Harbourside, and enjoyed a

The Chef's Touch

marvelous meal inspired by Tony's love of Italian cuisine. One of my fondest culinary memories of the trip is a plate of sautéed fresh prawns accompanied by a warm bean and potato salad. The smoothness of the potatoes contrasted beautifully with the slightly rough textured beans, all glistening from an herbed vinaigrette. Our salad here brings a bit more to the plate, but I must give Tony credit for the inspiration (by way of Italy, where he enjoyed the bean-potato combination at one of his favorite trattorias).

The Rosemary Vinaigrette recipe yields 1¼ cups. The vinaigrette may be kept at room temperature for several hours before using or refrigerated in a covered, noncorrosive container for 2 to 3 days. If refrigerated, return the vinaigrette to room temperature and whisk vigorously before using.

Because of the Italian inspiration for this salad, I think it appropriate that rosemary be the star of the vinaigrette. Indigenous to the Mediterranean area, this herb has a very pungent flavor and aroma, and can overpower some foods. So use fresh rosemary with a light hand, and use even more caution with dried rosemary. In this vinaigrette you may substitute ⅛ teaspoon of dried rosemary for the suggested ½ teaspoon of fresh.

Navy beans or Great Northern beans are outstanding with this salad. Or go Italianate and use cannellini beans: kidney-shaped beans with a pleasantly mild flavor and slightly mealy texture when cooked. Whatever you do, don't succumb to expediency and use canned cooked beans.

The crispy leeks can be removed from the oven after the original 30 minutes, held at room temperature for several hours, and then placed in a 200-degree-Fahrenheit oven for a few minutes before serving.

For crisp greens, separately spin-dry the washed arugula and spinach in a salad spinner.

Our method for curing and roasting the duck does not preserve the meat as is done when preparing the traditional confit of duck (in this method, the meat is cured and then cooked and preserved in its own fat). But it is delicious anyway. Unlike confit—which can be held for months—the cured and roasted duck meat can be kept refrigerated only for several days in a tightly sealed plastic container.

(continued on next page)

The Chef's Touch

For preparing lemon zest, use a sharp vegetable peeler to remove the skin from a lemon (being careful to remove only the colored part and not the bitter white pith under the skin), then use a very sharp cook's knife to cut the lemon peel into very thin strips.

Many varieties of wine would go with this salad, but yesterday's memory of an Iron Horse Sauvignon Blanc is still in mind. Crisp, with a light citrus undertone, this refreshing wine holds its own when paired with the less than bashful flavors of this salad. I also like the way this wine seems to cut through the slight oiliness of the vinaigrette.

Broccoli Bouquet with Garbanzo Bean and Tomato Relish, Spaghetti Squash, Chiffonade of Spinach, and Balsamic Vinaigrette

Serves 4

Balsamic Vinaigrette

4 tablespoons balsamic vinegar
2 tablespoons fresh lemon juice
1 cup extra-virgin olive oil

1 tablespoon chopped fresh oregano
salt and freshly ground black pepper to taste

Garbanzo Bean and Tomato Relish

1½ cups dried garbanzo beans (chickpeas),
    washed, picked over, and soaked for
    12 hours in 1 quart cold water
2 teaspoons salt
4 medium plum tomatoes (about 2 ounces
    each), washed, cored, and chopped into
    ¼-inch pieces

Balsamic Vinaigrette
salt and freshly ground black pepper to taste

Spaghetti Squash

1 medium spaghetti squash (3 to 3½ pounds)
2 cups water
4 tablespoons extra-virgin olive oil

1 tablespoon chopped fresh oregano
salt and freshly ground black pepper to taste

Equipment

measuring spoons
measuring cup
cook's knife
cutting board
colander
3-quart plastic container
paring knife
salad spinner
3-quart stainless steel bowl
whisk
plastic wrap
5-quart saucepan
5-quart stainless steel bowl
rubber spatula
paring knife
baking sheet with sides
metal kitchen spoon
7-quart stainless steel bowl
3-quart saucepan

Scallop variation requires:
slotted metal kitchen
    spoon

*Chicken sausage variation
    requires:*
small nonstick sauté pan
meat grinder with coarse
    grinding plate
medium nonstick sauté
    pan
paper towels

Salad Greens and Garnish

1 medium bunch broccoli (about 1 pound)
¼ pound flat-leaf spinach, stemmed, cut
    widthwise into ½-inch-wide strips, washed,
    and dried

ॐ

MAKE THE BALSAMIC VINAIGRETTE
In a 3-quart stainless steel bowl, whisk together the balsamic vinegar and lemon juice. Add the olive oil in a slow, steady stream while whisking until incorporated. Add the oregano, season with salt and pepper, and whisk to combine. Cover with plastic wrap and set aside at room temperature until needed.

PREPARE THE GARBANZO BEAN
AND TOMATO RELISH
Drain the soaked beans in a colander. Rinse the beans with cold water and drain thoroughly before cooking.

Bring 2 quarts of water and 2 teaspoons of salt to a boil in a 5-quart saucepan over high heat. Add the beans, adjust the heat, and simmer the beans about 45 minutes, until tender. Drain the beans in a colander, then transfer to a 5-quart stainless steel bowl. Add the plum tomatoes. Vigorously whisk the vinaigrette, then add ½ cup to the beans and tomatoes. (Cover the remaining ¾ cup of vinaigrette with plastic wrap and set aside at room temperature until needed.) Using a rubber spatula, stir the ingredients until combined. Season with salt and pepper. Cover the bowl with plastic wrap and set aside for up to 3 hours at room temperature. Or cool to room temperature and then refrigerate in a covered, noncorrosive container for up to 3 days before serving.

PREPARE THE SPAGHETTI SQUASH
Preheat the oven to 350 degrees Fahrenheit.

With the tip of a paring knife, make 8 to 10 random ½- to 1-inch-deep punctures in the sides of the spaghetti squash; this will allow the steam to escape from the squash and prevent it from rupturing while baking. Place the squash on a baking sheet with sides, add 1 cup of water to the sheet, and bake in the preheated oven for 1 hour and 10 minutes to 1 hour and 15 minutes. Add 1 more cup of water to the baking sheet after the first 30 minutes. To test the squash for doneness, penetrate the skin with a paring knife; the squash is done when it is easily penetrated to a depth of 1 to 1½ inches. Cool the squash under cold running water for 10 minutes.

When the squash is cool enough to handle, split it in half lengthwise. Use a metal kitchen spoon to scrape the seeds away from the center of each half; discard the seeds. Scrape the squash flesh away from the skin; discard the skin. Break up the flesh by hand into thin, spaghetti-like strands.

Place the spaghetti squash in a 7-quart stainless steel bowl. Drizzle the olive oil over the squash. Add the oregano. Season with salt and pepper, and combine thoroughly but not too energetically so as not to break the strands into small pieces. The squash may be used immediately or covered with plastic wrap and held at room temperature for up to 2 hours before serving. Or cool to room temperature and then refrigerate in a covered, noncorrosive container for up to 2 days before serving.

FINISH AND ASSEMBLE THE SALAD

Trim the broccoli into florets and discard the stem. Bring 2 quarts of lightly salted water to a boil in a 3-quart saucepan over medium-high heat. Cook the broccoli in the boiling salted water until tender but still crunchy, about 2½ to 3 minutes. Transfer to a colander and drain thoroughly, then submerge in ice water to stop the cooking. Drain the broccoli again. Set aside.

Divide and arrange the spinach strips in a ring near and around the outside edge of four 10- to 12-inch room-temperature plates. Place an equal amount of spaghetti squash on each plate inside the ring of spinach. Use a kitchen spoon to spread the spaghetti squash into a ring forming a well 3 to 3½ inches in diameter in the center of the squash. Place an equal amount of garbanzo bean and tomato relish in each well of squash and add the broccoli to top it off. Vigorously whisk the remaining ¾ cup of vinaigrette. Dress each salad with 2 to 3 tablespoons of the vinaigrette. Serve immediately.

❧

*W*arm *Marinated Scallops and Anchovies Variation*

1 pound sea scallops, side muscle removed
1 tablespoon extra-virgin olive oil
2 medium plum tomatoes (about 2 ounces each), cored, peeled, seeded, and finely chopped

salt and freshly ground black pepper to taste
½ cup sauvignon blanc or similar dry white wine
1 tablespoon fresh lemon juice
8 anchovies, chopped into ¼-inch pieces

Place the sea scallops in a 3-quart stainless steel bowl. Set aside for a few minutes.

Heat the olive oil in a 3-quart saucepan over medium heat. When the oil is hot, add the plum tomatoes and season with salt and pepper. Cook the tomatoes, stirring often, for 3 minutes. Add the wine and lemon juice, and bring to a boil. Pour the boiling mixture over the scallops in the bowl and stir to combine. Cover the bowl with plastic wrap and hold at room temperature for 10 minutes. Remove the plastic wrap, add the anchovies, and stir to combine. Use a slotted spoon to remove the scallop and anchovy mixture from the marinade and place an equal amount on each salad. Serve immediately.

❧

*C*hicken *Sausage Variation*

2 tablespoons extra-virgin olive oil
¼ cup minced onion
1 tablespoon finely chopped fresh parsley
½ teaspoon finely chopped fresh rosemary

1 pound boneless, skinless chicken breast, cut into 1-inch pieces
salt and freshly ground black pepper to taste

Heat 1 tablespoon of olive oil in a small nonstick sauté pan over medium-high heat. When the oil is hot, add the onion and cook about 2 minutes, until golden brown. Add the parsley and rosemary, and stir to combine. Transfer the mixture to a dish and place, uncovered, in the refrigerator to chill for 30 minutes.

Put the chicken pieces through a meat grinder fitted with a coarse grinding plate into a 3-quart stainless steel bowl. Add the cooled onion mixture and gently but thoroughly combine.

Gently form the chicken mixture into four 4-ounce patties, 1 inch thick. Cook immediately or cover with plastic wrap and refrigerate until needed (up to 24 hours).

Preheat the oven to 325 degrees Fahrenheit.

Season the patties with salt and pepper. Heat the remaining tablespoon of olive oil in a medium nonstick sauté pan over medium-high heat. When the oil is hot, add the patties and pan-sear for 2 minutes on each side, until golden brown. Transfer the patties to a nonstick baking sheet and place in the preheated oven for 15 minutes to finish cooking. Remove the patties from the oven and transfer to a large plate lined with paper towels. Keep on the plate for a minute or so to allow the towels to absorb the excess grease. Place a patty on each salad. Serve immediately.

The Chef's Touch

GARBANZO BEANS aren't what they used to be, thank goodness. My first encounter with garbanzo beans—a.k.a. chickpeas—was at Tad's Steak House in New York City during a high school trip in 1962. Tad's was a low-end restaurant in the heart of the Naked City (that was before the Big Apple was plucked) whose claim to fame was its cheap (read *gristly*) steak. The whole meal was $1.29, including baked potato, grilled bread, and a salad of iceberg lettuce topped with what looked like very shiny hazelnuts. Being a fan of hazelnuts, I plucked one off the tip of the iceberg. Imagine my disgust when I encountered a mushy and metallic mass instead of the expected crunchy and salty nut.

Hello, garbanzo bean in a can. The problem was that most people at that time thought garbanzo beans *originated* in a can. They soon popped up on salad bars across the country, still swimming in their briny canned stew. I vowed never to touch them again—and then sometime in the 80s at a trendy California restaurant I tried a dried version of the dreaded chickpea. Greetings, flavor and texture!

Dried garbanzo beans cook up to a slightly nutty and decidedly buttery flavor, and they are delicious. Please do not substitute canned garbanzo beans for the dried in this recipe.

(*continued on next page*)

The Chef's Touch

The Balsamic Vinaigrette recipe yields 1¼ cups. The vinaigrette may be kept at room temperature for 2 to 3 hours before using or refrigerated in a covered, noncorrosive container for 2 to 3 days. If refrigerated, return the vinaigrette to room temperature and whisk vigorously before using.

The spaghetti squash is magical. The bland exterior of this rather large vegetable belies its astounding and delicious interior, which when cooked yields golden, textural strands that are reminiscent of pasta. The squash can be baked as directed in this recipe, or it may be boiled. Cooking time varies depending on the size of the squash, and you can test for doneness using the same method as with baked squash.

When selecting spaghetti squash, choose a very hard one that doesn't give way to pressure when handled and with a smooth surface, devoid of blemishes. Also, the best squash feel heavy for their size, about 3 to 3½ pounds for an 8- to 10-inch-long squash.

The distinctive herbal flavor of fresh oregano becomes excessive when it is dried and will overwhelm this recipe. If fresh oregano is not available, other fresh herbs such as basil (use the same amount) or thyme and rosemary (use half the amount) will work well in this recipe. If you feel compelled to use dried oregano, use 1 teaspoon of dried oregano in place of 1 tablespoon of fresh.

One small bunch of flat-leaf spinach, about ¼ pound as purchased, should yield ⅛ pound of stemmed leaves. For crisp greens, spin-dry the washed spinach leaves in a salad spinner.

I suggest you ask your fish vendor whether the scallops available have been "dipped." This immersion in a solution of sodium tripolyphosphate extends the shelf life of fresh scallops and keeps them white. However, the "dip" also accomplishes a profound diminishment of fresh seafood flavor and makes the scallops rubbery. Rather than "dipped" scallops, look for "sticky" scallops; if fresh and untampered with, they will adhere to each other.

Although the garbanzo beans are distinctly buttery, I don't think it redundant to select a rich, round, and buttery chardonnay to accompany this salad. A Kistler Chardonnay (Sonoma Mountain, McCrea Vineyard) would join the tastes and textures of this salad in a triumphant food and wine pairing.

Marinated French Lentils with Grilled Vegetables, Curly Endive, and Walnut Oil Vinaigrette

Serves 4

Walnut Oil Vinaigrette

8 tablespoons red wine vinegar
2 tablespoons fresh lemon juice
1 tablespoon Dijon-style mustard
½ cup safflower oil

½ cup walnut oil
1 tablespoon chopped fresh parsley
salt and freshly ground black pepper to taste

Marinated French Lentils

1½ cups French green lentils, picked over,
    washed, and drained
1 teaspoon salt
1 tablespoon safflower oil
½ cup finely chopped onion

¼ cup finely chopped carrot
¼ cup finely chopped celery
¼ cup finely chopped red bell pepper
freshly ground black pepper to taste
Walnut Oil Vinaigrette

Grilled Vegetables

4 heads Belgian endive (about 1 pound),
    cut in quarters lengthwise, washed, and
    dried

4 tablespoons safflower oil
salt and freshly ground black pepper to taste
20 scallions, cleaned and trimmed

Salad Greens

¾ pound curly endive, cored, trimmed, cut
    into ¾-inch pieces, washed, and dried

Equipment

measuring spoons
measuring cup
cook's knife
cutting board
colander
paring knife
vegetable peeler
salad spinner
3-quart stainless steel bowl
whisk
plastic wrap
3-quart saucepan
medium nonstick sauté
  pan
7-quart stainless steel bowl
basting brush
charcoal grill
tongs
2 baking sheets

*Cured salmon variation
  requires:*
baking sheet with sides
paper towels
sharp slicer

Chicken variation requires:
5-quart plastic container
  with lid

MAKE THE WALNUT OIL VINAIGRETTE

In a 3-quart stainless steel bowl, whisk together the red wine vinegar, lemon juice, and Dijon mustard. Add the safflower oil and walnut oil, and whisk vigorously to combine. Add the parsley and whisk to combine. Season with salt and pepper. Cover tightly with plastic wrap and set aside at room temperature until needed.

PREPARE THE LENTILS

Place the lentils in a 3-quart saucepan and cover with 1½ quarts of cold water. Add 1 teaspoon of salt. Bring to a simmer over medium-high heat, then adjust the heat to continue to simmer until the lentils are cooked through but not mushy, about 30 to 35 minutes.

While the lentils are cooking, sauté the vegetables: Heat the safflower oil in a medium nonstick sauté pan over medium-high heat. When hot, add the onion, carrot, celery, and red bell pepper. Lightly season with salt and pepper, and sauté for 8 minutes, until tender and flavorful. Transfer the vegetables to a 7-quart stainless steel bowl and set aside until needed.

When the lentils are cooked, drain in a colander. Transfer the lentils to the 7-quart stainless steel bowl with the cooked vegetables. Whisk the vinaigrette, then add ½ cup to the bowl with the lentils and vegetables, and stir to incorporate. (Cover the remaining cup of vinaigrette with plastic wrap and set aside at room temperature until needed.) Cover tightly with plastic wrap and set aside at room temperature while grilling the vegetables.

GRILL THE VEGETABLES

Preheat the oven to 225 degrees Fahrenheit.

Brush the cut surfaces of the Belgian endive with 2 tablespoons of safflower oil. Season with salt and pepper. Grill over a medium wood or charcoal fire, turning frequently, about 4 to

5 minutes, until golden brown and tender. Transfer the grilled endive to a baking sheet and hold in the preheated oven while grilling the scallions.

Brush the scallions with the remaining 2 tablespoons of safflower oil and season generously with salt and pepper. Grill the scallions over a medium wood or charcoal fire about 3 to 4 minutes, until tender. Turn frequently to prevent them from burning. Transfer to a baking sheet and place in the preheated oven while assembling the salads.

ASSEMBLE THE SALAD

Divide and arrange the curly endive leaves in a ring on each of four 10- to 12-inch room-temperature plates. Place approximately 1 cup of the lentil mixture in the center of the ring of curly endive leaves. Artfully arrange 4 grilled Belgian endive quarters and 5 grilled scallions on each portion. Whisk the vinaigrette. Dress each salad with 3 to 4 tablespoons of the vinaigrette. Serve immediately.

*H*erb-Cured Salmon Variation

1 1-pound skinless fresh salmon fillet	2 tablespoons chopped fresh parsley
2 tablespoons brandy	1 tablespoon chopped fresh thyme
½ cup kosher salt	½ tablespoon chopped fresh oregano
2 tablespoons granulated sugar	
1 tablespoon freshly cracked black peppercorns	

Place the salmon fillet on one end of a large piece of plastic wrap that is twice as big as the fish. Place the fillet on a baking sheet with sides. Rub the brandy on the fillet, turning it over to coat both sides. Combine the kosher salt, sugar, and peppercorns. Sprinkle half of this mixture on the fillet, then turn over and sprinkle the remaining mixture on the other side, spreading evenly. Sprinkle the chopped herbs on one side of the fillet (preferably the side opposite the original skin side), spreading evenly to coat. Fold the plastic wrap over the top of the fillet. Cover the entire baking sheet with plastic wrap and refrigerate for at least 24 hours but no longer than 48 hours.

Remove the fillet from the refrigerator. Remove and discard the plastic wrap. Use your hands to gently brush the herbs off the fillet. Transfer the fillet to a baking sheet lined with paper towels. Pat the fillet dry with additional paper towels. Transfer the fillet to a cutting board and use a very sharp slicer to cut the fillet into paper-thin slices on a slight angle. Divide the slices into 4 equal portions and arrange on top of each salad. Serve immediately.

%

Mustard-Grilled Chicken Breast Variation

6 tablespoons Dijon-style mustard
4 tablespoons dry white wine
2 tablespoons whole-grain mustard

2 tablespoons sour cream
4 chicken breast halves with skin on
salt and freshly ground black pepper to taste

At least 1 day before serving, prepare the marinade by whisking together in a 3-quart stainless steel bowl the Dijon mustard, white wine, whole-grain mustard, and sour cream. Season the chicken breasts with salt and pepper. Place the chicken breasts in a 5-quart plastic container. Pour the marinade over the chicken and turn to coat thoroughly. Seal the container and refrigerate until ready to grill, at least 24 hours.

Preheat the oven to 350 degrees Fahrenheit.

Grill the chicken over a medium-hot wood or charcoal fire for 15 minutes. Turn the chicken as necessary to prevent overcharring. Transfer the breasts to a baking sheet and finish the cooking in the preheated oven for 15 minutes.

Place a chicken breast on each salad and serve immediately. The chicken may also be served at room temperature within 2 to 3 hours of grilling, or refrigerate the breasts once cool and keep refrigerated for 1 or 2 days before serving chilled.

The Chef's Touch

ALTHOUGH WINTER is not my favorite season, I always look forward to the foods that are evocative of cooler temperatures. This salad is a perfect amalgam of legumes, vegetables, and even nuts—all auguring the waning daylight and chilly days to come but comforting us with foods of substance.

The Chef's Touch

The Walnut Oil Vinaigrette recipe yields 1½ cups. The vinaigrette may be kept for several hours before using or refrigerated in a covered, noncorrosive container for 2 to 3 days. If refrigerated, return the vinaigrette to room temperature and whisk vigorously before using.

I rarely ascend the soap box to preach the merits of a particular ingredient versus the deficiencies of another. I make an exception with lentils. I find the common brown lentil to have limited taste and less than desirable texture compared to the French green lentil. The French varietal is nutty and maintains its shape when well cooked, and well cooked it should be; otherwise, the flavor does not fully develop. Then what do you do with the common brown lentil? At The Trellis we use lots of them in our thick lentil soup, where texture is not as relevant (the lentils can be soft to thicken the soup).

Belgian endive should be easy to locate at the market from early September through late May. Look for firm, unblemished heads that weigh about 3 to 4 ounces each.

One medium head of curly endive, about ¾ pound as purchased, should yield ½ pound of prepared greens. For crisp greens, spin-dry the washed curly endive in a salad spinner.

Add some delicious crunch to this salad by garnishing it with toasted walnuts. Toast 1 cup of walnuts in a 325-degree-Fahrenheit oven for 10 minutes. Cool the nuts to room temperature before sprinkling an equal amount on each salad.

This salad makes a great appetizer, especially when served with the cured salmon option. (I recommend you serve half the amount suggested for a main course.)

Be certain that the salmon is completely boneless, that it doesn't have any of the tiny, almost translucent, pin bones. If the fish purveyor hasn't already removed these little demons, you can easily do it using a pair of needle-nose pliers.

Once cured, the salmon will keep, tightly wrapped, in the refrigerator for several days.

A glass of California cabernet sauvignon would be just the tonic to take the chill out of a wintery day as well as enhance the myriad tastes and textures of this salad. Choose a wine with a slightly fruity aftertaste.

Panfried Black Turtle Bean Cakes with Avocado, Papaya, Strawberries, Jicama, Leaf Lettuce, and Peppered Honey-Lime Dressing

Serves 4

Black Turtle Bean Cakes

¾ pound dried black turtle beans, washed, picked over, and soaked for 12 hours in 2 quarts cold water

2 tablespoons salt

½ cup minced onion

1 tablespoon chopped fresh basil

1 tablespoon minced jalapeño pepper

2 teaspoons minced garlic

¼ cup all-purpose flour

4 tablespoons safflower oil (for panfrying the cakes)

Peppered Honey-Lime Dressing

2 tablespoons cider vinegar

2 tablespoons Key lime juice

1 tablespoon honey

1 teaspoon freshly cracked black peppercorns

¾ cup safflower oil

salt to taste

Root and Fruit

1 pound jicama

1 pint strawberries

2 medium papayas (about 1 pound)

2 medium, ripe avocados (about ¾ pound)

Peppered Honey-Lime Dressing

Salad Greens and Garnish

¾ pound leaf lettuce (green or red), cored,
  separated into leaves, washed, and dried
8 teaspoons sour cream
2 tablespoons chopped fresh chives

ॐ

PREPARE THE BLACK TURTLE BEAN CAKES

Drain the soaked beans in a colander. Rinse the beans with cold running water and drain thoroughly before cooking.

Bring 2 quarts of water and the salt to a boil in a 5-quart saucepan over high heat. Add the beans. Adjust the heat and simmer the beans until tender, about 1 hour. Drain the beans in a colander, then return them to the 5-quart saucepan. Cool the beans in the saucepan by running them under cold running water for 3 to 4 minutes. Drain the beans thoroughly, then transfer to a 7-quart stainless steel bowl. Add the onion, basil, jalapeño pepper, and garlic. Using your hands (I suggest wearing a pair of plastic food handler's gloves), crush the beans into a lumpy paste and thoroughly combine all the ingredients.

Form the mixture into 8 individual 4-ounce balls. Flatten each ball into a cake 3 inches in diameter and 1 inch thick. Lightly coat both sides of each cake with flour. Place the cakes on a baking sheet, cover with plastic wrap, and refrigerate until needed.

MAKE THE PEPPERED HONEY-LIME DRESSING

In a 3-quart stainless steel bowl, whisk together the cider vinegar, lime juice, honey, and peppercorns. Add the safflower oil in a slow, steady stream while whisking until incorporated. Season with salt. Cover tightly with plastic wrap and set aside at room temperature until needed.

Equipment

colander
3-quart plastic container
measuring spoons
paring knife
cook's knife
cutting board
measuring cup
5-quart saucepan
7-quart stainless steel bowl
plastic food handler's
  gloves
baking sheet
plastic wrap
3-quart stainless steel bowl
whisk
medium nonstick sauté
  pan
spatula
paper towels

Beef variation requires:
four 8- to 10-inch bamboo
  or metal skewers
charcoal grill
tongs

Grouper variation requires:
large nonstick sauté pan
parchment paper
slotted spatula

PREPARE THE ROOT AND FRUIT

Peel the jicama, then cut it into strips 3 inches long and ¼ inch thick. Place the jicama in a 7-quart stainless steel bowl.

Place the strawberries in a colander and spray them with lukewarm water. Shake the colander to remove excess water from the berries. Stem and then slice the berries ¼ inch thick. Place the sliced berries in the bowl with the jicama.

Peel, split, seed, and then cut the papayas into ½-inch dice. Place the papayas in the bowl with the jicama and strawberries.

Peel, pit, and then cut the avocados into ½-inch dice. Place in the bowl. Vigorously whisk—make that *very vigorously* because this dressing does not stay emulsified for very long after it is whisked—the peppered honey-lime dressing. Pour ½ cup of dressing over the root and fruit in the bowl. (Cover the remaining ½ cup of dressing with plastic wrap and set aside at room temperature until needed.) Toss very gently to combine. Cover the bowl with plastic wrap and refrigerate until needed (up to 3 or 4 hours).

FINISH AND ASSEMBLE THE SALAD

Preheat the oven to 350 degrees Fahrenheit.

Heat 2 tablespoons of the safflower oil in a medium nonstick sauté pan over medium heat. When the oil is hot, place 4 black bean cakes in the pan and cook for 4 minutes on each side, until uniformly golden brown. Place the panfried cakes on a baking sheet. Discard the oil in the pan, wipe clean with paper towels, and then repeat the panfrying procedure with the remaining 4 cakes. When all the cakes have been panfried and transferred to the baking sheet, place the sheet in the preheated oven and heat the cakes for 10 minutes. While the cakes are heating, assemble the salads.

Arrange and divide the leaf lettuce on four 10- to 12-inch room-temperature plates. Vigorously whisk the remaining ½ cup of peppered honey-lime dressing. Dress the greens on each plate with 2 tablespoons of dressing. Place an equal amount of root and fruit on the greens on each plate. Remove the hot black turtle bean cakes from the oven and place 2 cakes on each salad. Top each cake with 1 to 2 teaspoons of sour cream and garnish with chives. Serve immediately.

Grilled Fiery Beef Skewer Variation

2 tablespoons safflower oil
1 tablespoon freshly cracked black
  peppercorns
1 medium jalapeño pepper, roasted, peeled,
  seeded, and minced

¼ teaspoon ground cayenne pepper
1 pound trimmed beef tenderloin, cut into
  ½-inch cubes
salt to taste

In a 3-quart stainless steel bowl, whisk together the safflower oil, peppercorns, jalapeño, and cayenne pepper. Place the tenderloin cubes in the bowl and use a rubber spatula to combine the ingredients until the beef is coated with the oil and peppers. Divide the beef into 4 equal portions. Put each portion on a skewer. Season the beef with salt.

Grill the skewers over a medium wood or charcoal fire for 4 to 5 minutes for medium-rare and longer for more well done, turning as necessary to brown evenly. The beef skewers may also be cooked under the broiler in your oven. Broil for 6 minutes for medium-rare and longer for more well done, turning the skewers about halfway through the cooking time. Remove the beef from the skewers and place one portion on each salad. Serve immediately.

Tequila-Steamed Grouper Variation

4 4-ounce skinless grouper fillets
salt and freshly ground black pepper to taste
1 medium lime, washed and sliced into
  12 slices ⅛ inch thick

½ cup tequila
½ cup water
2 tablespoons Key lime juice

Season both sides of the grouper fillets with salt and pepper. Place 3 lime slices on top of each fillet.

Heat the tequila, water, and lime juice in a large nonstick sauté pan over medium-high heat. When the liquid begins to simmer, place the fillets, evenly spaced, in the pan. Cover the fish with a piece of parchment paper cut to fit the inside of the pan. Steam the fish fillets for 10 to 12 minutes, until cooked through. Use a slotted spatula to transfer the fillets to a baking sheet lined with paper towels to drain for a few seconds. Place a grouper fillet on each salad. Serve immediately.

The Chef's Touch

SOUTHWEST REGIONAL cooking came on the scene in a big way beginning in the late 70s. Since then, what used to be a mélange of influences from Mexican, American Indian, and even cowboy cooking has developed in flavor and sophistication in a fashion that is unparalleled vis-à-vis other American regional styles of cooking. The notable practitioners of the genre, chefs like Mark Miller, Dean Fearing, Stephan Pyles, and Robert Del Grande, have peppered their way into the forefront of the contemporary food scene. Other prominent chefs, such as Jeremiah Tower of San Francisco, took notice of this and incorporated southwestern influence into their kitchens. In the 80s, at Chef Tower's Santa Fe Bar & Grill in Berkeley, I tasted my first black bean cake (he reportedly invented this savory item). Our recipe is quite uncomplicated, but with a bean that delivers so much flavor, why get too fussy?

Routinely located in the bulk foods section at the supermarket, black beans have a characteristic sweet flavor and a smooth texture that enable the cook to use them in an abundance of ways. Black bean soup is a signature dish in scores of restaurants across the land. You will find black beans and rice being enjoyed hundreds of miles away from the island that put the dish on the map. And black beans in salads, relishes, and garnishes, and as a vegetable side dish, lend a colorful contrast on any table.

A little caution when handling chiles, by using plastic food handler's gloves, can prevent certain irritations (the seeds are especially potent). Or for those less sensitive, be sure to wash your hands after handling—and don't touch your eyes or other delicate areas until you do.

The Peppered Honey-Lime Dressing recipe yields about 1 cup. The dressing may be kept at room temperature for a couple of hours before using or refrigerated in a covered, noncorrosive container for up to 2 days. If refrigerated, return the dressing to room temperature and whisk vigorously before using.

I find that Nellie & Joe's Famous Key West Lime Juice (a bottled 100-percent natural juice) delivers a zingy flavor in dressings, marinades, or even confections. If your local supermarket doesn't carry it, you may substitute an equal amount of fresh lime juice (and, of course, if you have access to fresh Key limes, by all means use them).

Jicama usually can be found at the market year-round. I'm surprised at the number of uninitiated when it comes to this sweet-flavored root vegetable. I personally prefer jicama raw or barely warmed rather than cooked, especially since it tends to break apart when subjected to heat and handling. Select solid roots that have fairly smooth and relatively unblemished skins; also, choose the roots that weigh the heaviest for their particular size, meaning they are denser and will have better texture.

I hope you won't be intimidated by papayas. Although slightly strange in appearance, they are easy to render edible and deliver splendid flavor. Select fruit that has a minimum of green coloration (the more dominant its golden exterior, the sweeter the fruit). If your fruit is still green, ripen it at room temperature for a day or so.

One medium head of red or green leaf lettuce, about ¾ pound as purchased, should yield ½ pound of prepared greens. For crisp greens, spin-dry the washed lettuce leaves in a salad spinner.

The earthy and exotic qualities of this salad will commingle on your palate, and even more so with an extraordinary California Central Coast wine, Ojai Syrah. A hint of spice and a smooth round berry finish make this red wine approachable, drinkable, and enjoyable.

Fresh Garden Peas with Roasted Pearl Onions, Red Peppers, Bibb Lettuce, Cheddar Toasts, and Lemon Pepper Mayonnaise

Serves 4

Lemon Pepper Mayonnaise

1 cup mayonnaise
2 tablespoons fresh lemon juice

2 teaspoons freshly cracked black peppercorns

Vegetables

1 pound pearl onions, ends trimmed, peeled
3 tablespoons extra-virgin olive oil
salt and freshly ground black pepper to taste
2 pounds fresh garden peas in the pod, shelled
1 small red bell pepper (about ¼ pound), washed, cut in half lengthwise, core removed, seeded, membrane removed, and cut into thin strips the length of the pepper

2 tablespoons fresh lemon juice
2 teaspoons minced lemon zest
½ cup washed and dried Italian parsley leaves

Cheddar Toasts

½ cup minced onion
2 ounces sharp cheddar cheese, grated
2 tablespoons unsalted butter, softened

freshly ground black pepper to taste
16 slices ½-inch-thick French bread

Salad Greens

1 pound Bibb lettuce, cored, separated into leaves, washed, and dried

৳

MAKE THE LEMON PEPPER MAYONNAISE

In a 3-quart stainless steel bowl, vigorously whisk together the mayonnaise, lemon juice, and the peppercorns. Cover with plastic wrap and refrigerate until needed.

PREPARE THE VEGETABLES

Preheat the oven to 375 degrees Fahrenheit.

Place the pearl onions on a nonstick baking sheet with sides. Drizzle 1 tablespoon of olive oil over the onions. Sprinkle salt and pepper over the onions. Place the baking sheet on the center shelf in the preheated oven and roast the onions for 30 minutes, until browned and tender. Remove from the oven and cool to room temperature.

While the onions are roasting, bring 1½ quarts of lightly salted water to a simmer in a 3-quart saucepan over medium-high heat. When the water begins to simmer, add the shelled peas. Simmer the peas until cooked but not mushy, 5 to 6 minutes. Immediately drain the cooked peas in a colander, then plunge them in ice water. When the peas are cold, drain thoroughly.

In a 7-quart stainless steel bowl, use a rubber spatula to combine the roasted pearl onions, cooked peas, red bell pepper strips, lemon juice, remaining 2 tablespoons olive oil, and lemon zest. Season with salt and pepper. Add the Italian parsley and toss gently to combine. Cover the bowl with plastic wrap and keep at room temperature for up to 2 hours before serving or refrigerate in a covered, noncorrosive container for up to 24 hours.

MAKE THE CHEDDAR TOASTS

Preheat the oven to 350 degrees Fahrenheit.

In a 3-quart stainless steel bowl, use a rubber spatula to blend together the onion, cheddar cheese, and butter. Season with pepper and combine thoroughly.

Place the sliced French bread on a nonstick baking sheet. Place 1 heaping teaspoon of the cheese mixture on each slice of

Equipment

measuring cup
measuring spoons
paring knife
cook's knife
cutting board
vegetable peeler
box grater
serrated slicer
salad spinner
two 3-quart stainless steel
   bowls
whisk
plastic wrap
nonstick baking sheet
   with sides
3-quart saucepan
colander
7-quart stainless steel bowl
rubber spatula
small metal spatula

Frittata variation requires:
slotted kitchen spoon
paper towels
large nonstick sauté pan
9-inch nonstick pie tin

Chicken variation requires:
pie tin
medium nonstick sauté
   pan
tongs
paper towels

bread. Use a small spatula or a butter knife to spread the cheese mixture to the edges. Place the baking sheet on the center shelf in the preheated oven. Toast for 15 minutes, until well browned. Remove from the oven and set aside while assembling the salad.

ASSEMBLE THE SALAD

Divide and arrange the Bibb lettuce leaves on four 10- to 12-inch room-temperature plates. Spoon an equal amount of the pearl onion and pea mixture on each portion of salad. Dress each salad with 3 to 4 tablespoons of lemon pepper mayonnaise. Serve immediately accompanied by the cheddar toasts.

❧

Smoked Bacon and Onion Frittata Variation

¾ pound hickory-smoked slab bacon
1 teaspoon safflower oil
2 medium onions (about 1 pound), thinly
   sliced
salt and freshly ground black pepper to
   taste

4 large eggs
1 tablespoon chopped fresh Italian
   parsley

Preheat the oven to 350 degrees Fahrenheit.

Trim the rind and excess fat from the bacon. Slice the bacon into ½-inch-thick strips, then cut the strips into ½-inch dice. Place the diced bacon on a baking sheet with sides. Place the baking sheet on the center rack of the preheated oven and cook the bacon for 30 minutes, until well browned and crisp. Remove the bacon from the oven. Use a slotted spoon to transfer the bacon to a baking sheet lined with paper towels. Set aside until needed.

Heat the safflower oil in a large nonstick sauté pan over medium heat. When the oil is hot, add the onions. Season with salt and pepper. Cook, stirring occasionally, about 10 minutes, until the onions are tender. Transfer the onions to a baking sheet for a few minutes, to cool to room temperature.

In a 3-quart stainless steel bowl, whisk together the eggs and parsley. Add the bacon and onions, and stir to combine. Pour the mixture into a 9-inch nonstick pie tin and bake on the center rack of the preheated oven for 30 minutes, until lightly browned. Remove the frittata from the oven and cut into 4 equal wedges. Place a wedge on top of each salad. Serve immediately.

Panfried Buttermilk Chicken Variation

4 4-ounce boneless, skinless chicken breasts,
  each cut into 3 strips about 4 inches long
  and 1 inch wide
salt and freshly ground black pepper to taste

1 cup buttermilk
1 cup all-purpose flour
1 cup yellow cornmeal
1 cup peanut oil

Season the chicken strips with salt and pepper. Place the chicken in a 3-quart stainless steel bowl. Add the buttermilk and stir to coat. Cover the bowl with plastic wrap and refrigerate for 2 hours.

Preheat the oven to 225 degrees Fahrenheit.

Combine the flour and cornmeal in a pie tin. Season with salt and pepper.

Heat $\frac{1}{2}$ cup of peanut oil in a medium nonstick sauté pan over medium-high heat. While the oil is heating, remove the chicken strips from the buttermilk. Place the chicken strips in the flour and cornmeal mixture, coating each strip evenly and lightly. When the oil is very hot, add half the amount of chicken strips and panfry for about $1\frac{1}{2}$ minutes on each side, until golden brown and crispy. Transfer the fried chicken strips to a baking sheet lined with paper towels, and place in the preheated oven while frying the second batch of strips. Discard the oil and wipe out the pan with paper towels. Heat the remaining $\frac{1}{2}$ cup of peanut oil in the sauté pan over medium-high heat. Repeat the panfrying procedure with the remaining chicken strips. Transfer the second batch of strips to the paper-towel-lined baking sheet with the other strips. Keep at room temperature for 1 to 2 minutes (so the paper towels can absorb any excess grease) before placing 3 chicken strips on each salad. Serve immediately.

The Chef's Touch

THE early-nineteenth-century cookbook *The Virginia House-Wife* has been a source of culinary stimulus for me since I had access to a prized edition while working for the Colonial Williamsburg Foundation in the 70s. Now available in a facsimile edition with historical notes and commentaries by noted historian Karen Hess, it remains inspirational but affordable. Not only is it brimming

(continued on next page)

with interesting culinary lore, but it also offers compelling evidence that good cooking is not an invention of so-called new American chefs. Having said that, I might also add that the author's opinion is at once fanciful and then skeptical. Witness what Mrs. Randolph had to say about fresh peas: "To have them in perfection, they must be quite young, gathered early in the morning, kept in a cool place, and not shelled until they are to be dressed." She follows that statement with "boil them quick twenty or thirty minutes."

Fresh young peas directly out of the pod are sure to be sweet enough to eat raw, and a quick immersion in boiling water should make the fresh peas even better. Nevertheless, I suggest that you add the book to your collection the next time you visit Williamsburg. It is readily available at our local bookstores as well as at Colonial Williamsburg.

The Lemon Pepper Mayonnaise recipe yields about 1⅛ cups of dressing. The dressing may be stored, tightly covered, in a noncorrosive container in the refrigerator for 2 to 3 days.

Zesting citrus fruit can be accomplished using a vegetable peeler and a sharp cook's knife. Use the peeler to remove the colored skin from the fruit, being careful to remove only the skin and not the bitter white pith that is directly underneath. Use a cook's knife to cut the skin into very fine julienne strips, then finely mince the julienne strips.

If Italian parsley (also called flat-leaf parsley) is not available, you may substitute the more prosaic and readily available curly leaf parsley. The Italian parsley has a slightly more assertive flavor, but I like it for its larger leaves, especially when used as we have for this salad.

Two medium heads of Bibb lettuce, each weighing about ½ pound as purchased, should yield ¾ pound of prepared lettuce. For crisp greens, spin-dry the washed Bibb lettuce in a salad spinner.

According to "the book," a frittata is never baked; it is cooked slowly in a pan. If it is baked, it is called a tortino. So if you're fussy about details like this, you should call our frittata a tortino!

My palate prefers the crisp, clean taste of a sauvignon blanc wine at lunch more than an overly stylized chardonnay that one must chew rather than sip. A light and fruity Cakebread Sauvignon Blanc would be a refreshing choice with this salad and its variations.

Grains

Roasted Corn, Okra, and Pepper Relish with Corn Pasta, Red Leaf Lettuce, and Guacamole Dressing

Serves 4

Corn Pasta

1½ cups all-purpose flour
½ cup masa harina
1 teaspoon ground cumin
1 teaspoon salt

3 large eggs
3 tablespoons corn oil
salt and freshly ground black pepper to taste

Roasted Corn, Okra, and Pepper Relish

4 ears fresh corn (about 2 pounds), husk and silk removed
3 tablespoons corn oil
salt and freshly ground black pepper to taste
1 cup unsalted peanuts
1 tablespoon minced jalapeño pepper
1 pound okra, washed, stems trimmed, and cut widthwise into ½-inch pieces
½ cup sauvignon blanc or similar dry white wine
1 cup chopped scallions (about 1 bunch with root ends trimmed)

1 medium red bell pepper (about 6 ounces), roasted, peeled, cut in half lengthwise, seeded, and cut into ½-inch dice
2 medium Anaheim chili peppers (about 3 ounces), roasted, peeled, cut in half lengthwise, seeded, and cut across the width into ⅛-inch-wide strips
1 tablespoon fresh chopped cilantro
1 tablespoon fresh lime juice

Equipment

measuring cup
measuring spoons
cook's knife
cutting board
tongs
salad spinner
plastic wrap
baking sheet
two 7-quart bowls
large nonstick sauté pan
rubber spatula
food processor with metal
    blade
pasta machine
5-quart saucepan
colander

*Panfried crabcake variation
    requires:*
3-quart stainless steel bowl
whisk
medium nonstick sauté
    pan
spatula

*Smoked sausage variation
    requires:*
medium nonstick sauté
    pan

Guacamole Dressing

1 medium avocado (about 6 ounces)
2 tablespoons cider vinegar
1 tablespoon fresh lime juice
¼ cup sour cream
2 tablespoons tequila
⅛ teaspoon ground cayenne pepper
salt to taste

Salad Greens

¾ pound red leaf lettuce, cored, separated
    into leaves, washed, and dried

PREPARE THE CORN PASTA DOUGH

Combine 1¼ cups of flour, masa harina, cumin, and 1 teaspoon of salt on a clean, dry work surface or in a 7-quart bowl. Make a well in the center of the flour mixture large enough to hold the eggs and 1 tablespoon of corn oil. (The remaining 2 tablespoons will be used to coat the cooked pasta.) Using a fork, thoroughly combine the eggs and oil, then gradually work the flour into the egg mixture, a small amount at a time. Once the dough is stiff enough to handle, begin kneading by hand. Knead until all the flour has been incorporated, about 10 minutes. Wrap the dough in plastic wrap and set aside at room temperature for 1½ to 2 hours while you make the relish and the dressing.

MAKE THE ROASTED CORN, OKRA,
AND PEPPER RELISH

Preheat the oven to 400 degrees Fahrenheit.

Place the ears of corn on a baking sheet. Brush the corn with 2 tablespoons of corn oil. Season liberally with salt and pepper. Place the baking sheet in the preheated oven and roast the corn for 40 minutes, until partially golden brown. Remove from the oven. Lower the oven temperature to 325 degrees Fahrenheit. When the corn is cool enough to handle, cut away the kernels. Place the kernels in a 7-quart stainless steel bowl and set aside at room temperature until needed.

Toast the peanuts on a baking sheet in the preheated 325-degree-Fahrenheit oven for

10 to 12 minutes, until golden brown. Remove the peanuts from the oven and set aside at room temperature to cool.

Heat the remaining 1 tablespoon of corn oil in a large nonstick sauté pan over medium-high heat. When the oil is hot, add the minced jalapeño pepper and cook for 30 seconds. Add the okra and wine, season with salt, and cook, stirring frequently, for 3½ to 4 minutes, until the okra tastes cooked but is still quite crunchy. Remove from the heat and transfer to the bowl with the corn, then add the scallions, red bell pepper, Anaheim chili pepper strips, cilantro, and lime juice. Stir to combine. Allow the mixture to cool, uncovered, at room temperature for 30 minutes. Add the peanuts and stir to combine. Cover the bowl with plastic wrap and set aside at room temperature for up to 3 hours before serving.

MAKE THE GUACAMOLE DRESSING

Cut, pit, peel, and then chop the avocado into 1-inch pieces. Place the avocado, cider vinegar, and 1 tablespoon of lime juice in the bowl of a food processor fitted with a metal blade. Pulse the ingredients for 30 seconds, then use a rubber spatula to scrape down the sides of the bowl. Process the mixture for another 30 seconds, until fairly smooth. Add the sour cream, tequila, and cayenne pepper, and process for 1 minute, until smooth. Season with salt. Transfer the dressing to a noncorrosive container, cover with plastic wrap, and refrigerate until needed.

CUT AND COOK THE CORN PASTA

Cut the pasta dough into 4 equal pieces. Roll and knead each piece of dough through the pasta machine, using the remaining ¼ cup of flour as necessary to prevent the dough from becoming sticky. Cut each sheet of dough into long thin strips of fettuccine.

Bring 3 quarts of salted water to a boil in a 5-quart saucepan over high heat. Add the pasta and cook, stirring frequently, about 1 minute, until tender but slightly firm to the bite. Drain the cooked pasta in a colander, then shake the colander to remove as much excess water from the pasta as possible. Transfer the well-drained pasta to a 7-quart stainless steel bowl. Drizzle 2 tablespoons of corn oil over the pasta, season with salt and pepper, and toss to coat the pasta with the oil. Cover loosely with plastic wrap and set aside for up to 1 hour before serving.

ASSEMBLE THE SALAD

Divide and arrange the red leaf lettuce leaves on four 10- to 12-inch room-temperature plates. Drizzle (we use a squeeze bottle at The Trellis) about 2 tablespoons of guacamole dressing over the lettuce on each plate. Place an equal amount of corn pasta on each portion of dressed lettuce. Create a well in the center of the pasta about 3½ inches in diameter. Place an equal amount of roasted corn, okra, and pepper relish inside each well of pasta. Drizzle 1 to 2 tablespoons of dressing over the relish. Serve immediately.

🦎

Panfried Crabcake Variation

2 tablespoons mayonnaise
1 teaspoon Dijon-style mustard
1 teaspoon fresh lemon juice
1 teaspoon hot sauce
1/8 teaspoon ground cayenne pepper

1 pound lump backfin crabmeat, well
  picked of shells
2 tablespoons minced fresh chives
salt to taste
1 tablespoon corn oil

In a 3-quart stainless steel bowl, whisk together the mayonnaise, mustard, lemon juice, hot sauce, and cayenne pepper until smooth. Add the crabmeat and chives, season with salt, then gently but thoroughly combine. Form the mixture into 4 cakes approximately 4 ounces and about 1 inch thick. Cover with plastic wrap and refrigerate for at least 30 minutes (and up to 24 hours) before cooking.

Preheat the oven to 300 degrees Fahrenheit.

Heat the corn oil in a medium nonstick sauté pan over medium heat. When the oil is hot, panfry the cakes for 4 minutes on each side, until golden brown. Transfer the cakes to a nonstick baking sheet and place in the preheated oven for 10 minutes, until hot throughout. Remove the crabcakes from the oven and place 1 on each salad. Serve immediately.

🦎

Smoked Sausage Variation

4 links smoked sausage, cut widthwise into
  1/2-inch-thick slices
3/4 cup finely chopped onion
1 teaspoon ground cumin

freshly ground black pepper to taste
1 medium tomato (about 6 ounces), peeled,
  seeded, and chopped into 1/4-inch pieces

Heat a medium nonstick sauté pan over medium-high heat. When the pan is hot, add the sausage and cook until browned, about 3 minutes. Add the onion and cumin, season with pepper, and continue to cook for 1 minute. Add the tomato and cook, stirring often, for 5 minutes, until thickened. Remove from the heat, then place an equal amount on each salad. Serve immediately.

The Chef's Touch

BETTY FUSSELL'S book *The Story of Corn* is a fitting paean to this most versatile of grains. The book reads like a novel, covering the mystery and spirituality, greed and commerce, religion and reproduction, and, of course, edibility of corn. The latter interests us most at the moment, but I recommend Fussell's book on all levels.

Masa harina, or corn flour, provides a singular flavor to our corn pasta. Cornmeal is not an appropriate substitute. You can find corn flour in the baking section of the supermarket as well as in the international section. After using the amount required for this recipe, I recommend storing the corn flour in a tightly sealed plastic container in the refrigerator; it will keep for months stored this way.

For advance preparation of the corn pasta, toss the cut pasta with ½ cup of cornmeal to prevent the strands from sticking to each other during refrigeration, then place the pasta on a baking sheet lined with parchment paper. Cover tightly with plastic wrap and refrigerate until ready to cook, up to 3 days. Be sure to shake the cornmeal off the pasta before cooking it in boiling water.

Roasting corn in or out of the husk provides two very different results. For this recipe I chose to remove the husk, which produces a drier, caramel-flavored corn. Corn roasted in the husk is more moist and has a smokier flavor.

Edible green okra pods are usually found year-round in markets in the South, where this odd vegetable is much beloved. The slippery texture of okra results from its secretion of mucilage, a gummy substance prevalent in certain plants (the marshmallow plant is another such example). There is no escaping this texture once okra is cut and cooked, but I have found that the longer okra is cooked, the slimier it gets: So don't overcook it, and it will be delicious.

The seeds and membrane inside the jalapeño pepper will be as hot or hotter

(*continued on next page*)

to your skin as they are to your palate, so be careful not to touch the chili and then your eyes or other sensitive areas. Wash your hands immediately after handling chiles or, better yet, wear a pair of plastic food handler's gloves to avoid contact completely.

If you refrigerate the Roasted Corn, Okra, and Pepper Relish, the peanuts will lose their crunch overnight. Another suggestion is to prepare the relish without the peanuts, refrigerate in a covered, noncorrosive container for up to 3 days, and then fold in the peanuts just before serving.

The Guacamole Dressing recipe yields about 1 cup. The dressing should be stored in a covered, noncorrosive container in the refrigerator for no more than 24 hours. Although the lime juice in this recipe helps prevent the avocado from oxidizing (contact with air discolors the flesh), in the dressing this effect is not long lasting. Like traditional guacamole, the dressing is best enjoyed within 2 to 3 hours of preparation, both for aesthetics and flavor.

One medium head of red leaf lettuce, about ¾ pound as purchased, should yield ½ pound of prepared lettuce leaves. For crisp greens, spin-dry the washed leaves in a lettuce spinner.

The smoked sausage we use at The Trellis is obtained from S. Wallace Edwards & Sons in Surry, Virginia. You may use your favorite sausage, but the Edwards hickory-smoked sausage contains no filler, has a moist texture, and is perfectly smoked the old-fashioned way (by real smoke, not chemicals).

I'm a big fan of sauvignon blanc wines. They are easy to drink and complement a variety of foods. Frog's Leap is one of my favorites, with vibrant flavors that don't confuse the palate with complex and vegetal nuances.

*B*ow Tie Pasta, Tangerines, Black Olives, and Grilled Red Onions with Olive Oil Dressing

Serves 4

Olive Oil Dressing

2 tablespoons red wine vinegar
1 tablespoon Dijon-style mustard
$\frac{1}{2}$ tablespoon fresh lemon juice
$\frac{1}{2}$ cup extra-virgin olive oil

1 tablespoon chopped fresh parsley
1 tablespoon chopped fresh tarragon
salt and freshly ground black pepper to taste

Pasta

2 large red onions (about 1 pound), peeled
   and sliced $\frac{3}{8}$ inch thick
6 tablespoons extra-virgin olive oil
salt and freshly ground black pepper to taste
1 pound bow tie pasta

4 tangerines, peeled, segmented, seeded,
   and cut into 1-inch pieces
48 Mediterranean black olives, pitted and
   chopped

Salad Greens and Garnish

$\frac{3}{4}$ pound red leaf lettuce, cored,
   separated into leaves, washed, and
   dried

$\frac{3}{4}$ pound flat-leaf spinach, stemmed,
   washed, and dried
4 teaspoons chopped fresh tarragon

§

MAKE THE OLIVE OIL DRESSING

Whisk together in a 3-quart stainless steel bowl the red wine vinegar, mustard, and lemon juice. Add the olive oil in a slow, steady stream while whisking until incorporated. Add the parsley, tarragon, salt, and pepper, and whisk to combine. Cover tightly with plastic wrap and set aside at room temperature.

PREPARE THE PASTA

Brush the red onion slices with 2 tablespoons of olive oil and season generously with salt and pepper. Grill the onion slices over a medium wood or charcoal fire about 6 minutes on each side, until nicely charred and tender. (The onions may also be cooked by broiling in the oven on a baking sheet until browned and tender.) Transfer the onions to a baking sheet and cool to room temperature. When the onions are cool enough to handle, cut each slice into ½-inch pieces. Set aside until needed.

Bring 3 quarts of salted water to a boil in a 5-quart saucepan over high heat. When boiling, add the bow tie pasta and cook, stirring frequently, about 12 minutes, until tender but firm to the bite. Drain the pasta in a colander, then cool with cold water. Drain thoroughly. Transfer the pasta to a 7-quart stainless steel bowl and add the remaining 4 tablespoons of olive oil. Toss to coat the pasta. Season with salt and pepper. Add the grilled onions, tangerine pieces, and olives. Use a rubber spatula to combine. Cover with plastic wrap and keep at room temperature for up to 2 hours before serving.

ASSEMBLE THE SALAD

Divide and arrange the red leaf lettuce leaves on four 10- to 12-inch room-temperature plates. Divide and arrange the spinach leaves on top of the red leaf lettuce. Vigorously whisk the olive oil dressing. Drizzle each portion of greens with 2 to 3 tablespoons of dressing. Place an equal amount of pasta on each plate of greens. Sprinkle 1 teaspoon of chopped tarragon on each salad. Serve immediately.

*

*M*ustard-Grilled Tuna Variation

4 tablespoons vegetable oil

2 tablespoons whole-grain mustard

1 tablespoon fresh orange juice

4 4- to 5-ounce tuna fillets, about ¾ inch
    thick

salt and freshly ground black pepper to taste

In a 1-quart stainless steel bowl, whisk together the vegetable oil, mustard, and orange juice until combined, then liberally brush the tuna fillets with the mixture. Season both sides of each fillet with salt and pepper. Cook immediately or cover each fillet with plastic wrap and refrigerate until needed (up to 24 hours).

Grill the tuna fillets over a medium wood or charcoal fire for 2 minutes on each side for medium rare; cook longer if more well done tuna is desired. (The tuna may also be pan-seared in a large nonstick sauté pan over medium-high heat. Cook for about the same amount of time as listed for grilling.) Place a tuna fillet onto each salad. Serve immediately.

*

*P*an-Seared Peppered Veal Medallion Variation

1 pound well-trimmed boneless veal
    loin, cut into 16 medallions ¼ inch
    thick

1 to 2 tablespoons freshly cracked black
    peppercorns

salt to taste

2 tablespoons extra-virgin olive oil

Generously sprinkle each side of the veal medallions with the peppercorns. Season lightly with salt. Heat 1 tablespoon of olive oil in each of 2 large nonstick sauté pans over medium-high heat. When the oil is hot, place 8 medallions in each pan and cook for 30 seconds on each side for medium-rare; cook longer if more well done meat is desired. Remove the medallions from the sauté pans and transfer to a baking sheet to cool for 2 to 3 minutes. Place 4 medallions on each salad. Serve immediately.

The Chef's Touch

A s   A   professional cook, whenever I see or think of bow ties—even bow tie pasta—I visualize the late dean of cooking, James Beard. The bow tie became Mr. Beard's sartorial trademark. But more important, his love of food expressed through his teaching, writings, and now his disciples is in part responsible for the renaissance of food in America during the last two decades. Since his passing, the James Beard Foundation celebrates Mr. Beard's birthday with various fetes across the country. For the last ten years at The Trellis we have dedicated our annual Virginia Vintner's Barrel Tasting and Dinner to James Beard. This salad is based on one of the courses we served at the Barrel Tasting in 1989.

The Olive Oil Dressing recipe yields about ¾ cup. The dressing may be kept at room temperature for several hours before using or refrigerated in a covered, noncorrosive container for 2 to 3 days. If refrigerated, return the dressing to room temperature and whisk vigorously before using.

I prefer the De Cecco brand of dried pasta from Italy. Made with high-quality durum wheat, this pasta maintains its shape after cooking and delivers a flavor and texture you won't find in many other boxed pastas.

If you are unable to locate tangerines (they may be difficult to find during most of the summer season), substitute a segmented seedless sweet orange.

Without disparaging other black olives, I highly recommend selecting the best-quality tree-ripened French or Greek black olives you can find. I stress *best* quality since a plethora of inferior olives is sold under the aegis of being Mediterranean. Ask your specialty grocer for a recommendation.

One medium head of red leaf lettuce, about ¾ pound as purchased, should yield ½ pound of prepared lettuce. And one large bunch of flat-leaf spinach, about ¾ pound as purchased, should yield ½ pound of stemmed leaves. For crisp greens, separately spin-dry the washed red leaf lettuce and washed spinach leaves in a salad spinner.

For smaller appetites you could get 6 servings from the pasta salad, but not around my house.

To work with an aggressively flavored dressing as well as the assertive flavor of the olives, I suggest a red wine that is not bashful with fruit but also does not dull the palate with residual sweetness. A smooth California cabernet sauvignon crafted by the Cakebread family would be my choice.

Warm Grilled Eggplant, Scallions, and Plum Tomatoes with Leaf Spinach, Warm Herbed Couscous, and a Roasted Garlic Dressing

Serves 4

Roasted Garlic Dressing

2 large cloves garlic, unpeeled
½ tablespoon extra-virgin olive oil
salt and freshly ground black pepper to taste
2 tablespoons finely minced onion

1 tablespoon Dijon-style mustard
¼ cup cider vinegar
1½ cups lowfat yogurt

Grilled Vegetables

1 medium eggplant (about 1¼ pounds), washed and cut widthwise into 16 slices ½ inch thick
6 large plum tomatoes, washed, cored, and cut in half lengthwise

16 scallions, cleaned and trimmed
¼ cup extra-virgin olive oil
salt and freshly ground black pepper to taste

Herbed Couscous

1 cup Vegetable Stock (see page 26)
1 tablespoon extra-virgin olive oil
½ teaspoon salt
¼ teaspoon ground white pepper

1 cup instant couscous
1 tablespoon chopped fresh parsley
½ tablespoon chopped fresh thyme
½ teaspoon chopped fresh oregano

Salad Greens

¾ pound flat-leaf spinach, stemmed, washed, and dried

§

MAKE THE ROASTED GARLIC DRESSING

Preheat the oven to 325 degrees Fahrenheit.

Place the garlic in a pie tin or small baking dish, sprinkle with the olive oil, and season lightly with salt and pepper. Cover the pie tin with aluminum foil. Place in the preheated oven and roast the garlic until tender, about 30 minutes. Remove the garlic from the oven, discard the aluminum foil, and cool to room temperature. When the garlic is cool enough to handle, peel and trim the cloves (the pulp should literally slide away from the skin), then finely chop the pulp. Place the chopped garlic into a 3-quart stainless steel bowl, along with the onion, mustard, and cider vinegar. Stir to combine. Add the yogurt and whisk until smooth. Cover tightly with plastic wrap and refrigerate until needed.

GRILL THE VEGETABLES

Preheat the oven to 200 degrees Fahrenheit.

Prior to grilling, liberally brush the vegetables with the olive oil and season generously with salt and pepper. Grill the eggplant slices over a medium wood or charcoal fire about 4 to 6 minutes on each side, until golden brown. Transfer to a baking sheet. Grill the tomato halves, cut side down, until nicely charred, about $3\frac{1}{2}$ to 4 minutes, then turn and grill on the opposite side for $1\frac{1}{2}$ to 2 minutes. Transfer to another baking sheet. Grill the scallions about 3 to 4 minutes, until tender, turning often to prevent overcharring. Transfer to a baking sheet. Place the baking sheets with the grilled vegetables in the preheated oven and keep warm while preparing the couscous.

PREPARE THE COUSCOUS

Combine the vegetable stock, olive oil, salt, and pepper in a 3-quart saucepan and bring to a boil over medium-high heat. Add the couscous to the boiling stock and stir to combine. Remove from the heat, cover with a lid or aluminum foil, and set aside for 5 minutes. Using a fork, stir the herbs into the couscous.

ASSEMBLE THE SALAD

Divide and arrange the spinach leaves on four 10- to 12-inch room-temperature plates. Sprinkle the spinach with 2 to 3 tablespoons of dressing. Place ¾ cup of couscous on the center of the spinach on each plate. Remove the grilled vegetables from the oven. Arrange 3 to 4 slices of eggplant, 3 plum tomato halves, and 4 grilled scallions around the mound of couscous on each plate. Sprinkle the couscous and grilled vegetables with 2 to 3 tablespoons of the dressing. Serve immediately.

Skewer of Fresh Sausage Variation

4 links fresh pork sausage
2 tablespoons water
12 fresh small shiitake mushrooms (about 6 ounces), stems removed
1 medium green bell pepper (about 6 ounces), washed, cut in half lengthwise, core removed, seeded, membrane removed, and cut into twelve 1-inch squares

1 medium red bell pepper (about 6 ounces), washed, cut in half lengthwise, core removed, seeded, membrane removed, and cut into twelve 1-inch squares
2 tablespoons extra-virgin olive oil
1 tablespoon chopped fresh parsley
salt and freshly ground black pepper to taste

Preheat the oven to 300 degrees Fahrenheit.

Place the sausage links in a pie tin. Puncture each sausage several times with a fork (the puncturing prevents the links from splitting apart in the oven). Add the water to the pie tin. Place in the preheated oven and cook the sausage for 30 minutes. Remove from the oven. Use a pair of tongs to transfer the sausage to a large plate lined with paper towels. Hold the sausage at room temperature for a few minutes, until any excess grease is absorbed by the paper towels.

Raise the oven to broil.

Cut each link of sausage into 4 pieces. Skewer 4 pieces of sausage on each skewer, alternating with 3 mushroom caps and 3 pieces of each color pepper. In a small bowl, whisk together the olive oil and parsley. Baste the skewers with the olive oil–parsley mixture. Season with salt and pepper. Broil the sausage skewers on a pie tin under the preheated broiler for 10 minutes, turning about halfway through the broiling time.

Remove the skewers from the oven and transfer to a plate lined with paper towels for a few minutes (to allow the towels to absorb any excess grease) before removing each portion from the skewers and positioning on each salad. Serve immediately.

ஃ

*P*an-Seared Rainbow Trout Variation

2 tablespoons fresh lemon juice

4 4- to 5-ounce rainbow trout fillets with
  skin on

salt and freshly ground black pepper to taste

1 teaspoon extra-virgin olive oil

Sprinkle the lemon juice on both sides of the trout fillets, then lightly season each side with salt and pepper. Cook immediately or individually wrap each fillet in plastic and refrigerate until needed (up to 24 hours).

Heat a large nonstick sauté pan over medium-high heat. When hot, brush the pan with the olive oil. Place 4 trout fillets in the pan skin side down, and sear for 3 to 4 minutes, until golden brown and crisp. Turn the fillets and cook for 1 minute on the other side. Remove the fillets from the pan and place 1 fillet, skin side up, on top of the couscous on each plate. Serve immediately.

The Chef's Touch

NOT FULLY understanding the tumultuous history that is Sicily's legacy, I was not prepared for the exotic foods I savored there on my first visit many years ago. I have delicious memories of an aromatic fish couscous that belied my prior notions of a simple dish. The warm, salty breeze only served to heighten that day's contentment. I would be less than honest if I failed to mention that the couscous was prepared in the traditional manner using long-cooking couscous. Most of us have precious few languorous days to enjoy warm, salty breezes. But since that should not affect our desire for good food, especially when prepared simply and relatively quickly, I can unequivocally recommend the use of instant couscous.

The Roasted Garlic Dressing recipe yields 2 cups. The dressing may be stored in a covered, noncorrosive container in the refrigerator for 3 to 4 days. For a richer dressing or if you are not a yogurt fan, substitute an equal amount of mayonnaise.

Look for boxed instant couscous (granular semolina) in the gourmet section at your supermarket or at a specialty grocer.

One large bunch of flat-leaf spinach, about ¾ pound as purchased, should yield ½ pound of stemmed leaves. Curly spinach may be substituted if flat-leaf is not available. Although I prefer the taste, texture, and appearance of flat-leaf spinach, I am also like Popeye—I love spinach flat or curly! For crisp greens, spin-dry the washed spinach leaves in a salad spinner.

The grilled vegetables may be served at room temperature. If that's your preference, then cool the vegetables to room temperature after grilling, cover loosely with plastic wrap, and keep at room temperature for 3 to 4 hours before serving. (If the weather outside is frightful, you may cook the vegetables by broiling in the oven until nicely charred.)

Although I prefer the couscous warm, it is also delicious at room temperature. If you choose the latter, cover the couscous with plastic wrap after it has cooled to room temperature. You can hold it at room temperature up to 4 hours before serving.

This salad also makes an excellent appetizer. As an appetizer, I would recommend serving half or even a third of the portion noted above.

A light red Valpolicella would work well with this salad and either of the options. Select a charming Valpolicella Classico Superiore, and you will transport your senses even without the warm, salty breeze.

Mandarin Orange Basmati Rice with Sesame Stir-Fried Vegetables, Tangy Red Cabbage, and Szechuan Peppercorn Vinaigrette

Serves 4

Tangy Red Cabbage

2 tablespoons red wine vinegar

1 tablespoon rice wine vinegar

1 tablespoon peanut oil

½ teaspoon minced garlic

½ teaspoon minced fresh ginger

½ teaspoon salt

½ small head red cabbage (about ¾ to 1 pound), discolored and tough outer leaves removed, washed, cored, quartered, and thinly sliced

1 small red onion (about 4 ounces), peeled and thinly sliced

Szechuan Peppercorn Vinaigrette

1 tablespoon Szechuan peppercorns

¼ cup rice wine vinegar

2 tablespoons soy sauce

¾ cup peanut oil

Mandarin Orange Basmati Rice

2 teaspoons peanut oil

1 cup white basmati rice

salt and freshly ground black pepper to taste

1¾ cups hot Vegetable Stock (see page 26)

2 tablespoons rice wine

Szechuan Peppercorn Vinaigrette

1 cup mandarin orange sections

Sesame Stir-Fried Vegetables

3 tablespoons sesame seeds
½ pound snow peas, trimmed
1 tablespoon peanut oil
1 teaspoon sesame oil
1 bunch scallions, cleaned, trimmed, and
     thinly sliced on the bias
½ medium head bok choy (about
     1½ pounds), cored, sliced ¼ inch thick
     (white part only), and washed
½ pound fresh water chestnuts, peeled and
     sliced ⅛ inch thick
salt and freshly ground black pepper to taste

Salad Greens

¾ pound Boston lettuce, cored, separated
     into leaves, washed, and dried

Equipment

measuring spoons
paring knife
cook's knife
cutting board
measuring cup
salad spinner
1½-quart saucepan
two 5-quart stainless steel
     bowls
plastic wrap
pie tin
spice grinder (coffee
     grinder)
3-quart stainless steel bowl
whisk
3-quart saucepan with lid
7-quart stainless steel bowl
rubber spatula
baking sheet
5-quart saucepan
colander
large nonstick sauté pan

Catfish variation requires:
charcoal grill
spatula
basting brush

*Flank steak variation
     requires:*
tongs
slicer

PREPARE THE TANGY RED CABBAGE
Heat the red wine vinegar, rice wine vinegar, peanut oil, garlic, ginger, and salt in a 1½-quart saucepan over medium-high heat. Bring to a boil. Place the cabbage and onion in a 5-quart stainless steel bowl. Pour the boiling marinade over the cabbage and onion, immediately cover the top of the bowl tightly with plastic wrap, and refrigerate for at least 1 hour (and up to 24 hours) before serving.

MAKE THE SZECHUAN PEPPERCORN VINAIGRETTE
Preheat the oven to 325 degrees Fahrenheit.
Toast the Szechuan peppercorns on a pie tin in the preheated oven for 5 minutes. Remove the peppercorns from the oven and cool to room temperature. Once cooled, finely grind the peppercorns in a spice or coffee grinder.
In a 3-quart stainless steel bowl, whisk together the rice wine vinegar, soy sauce, and peppercorns. Add the peanut oil in a slow, steady stream while whisking until incorporated. The vinaigrette will probably not need additional salt and pepper, but do taste it

and add additional seasoning if necessary. Cover the bowl with plastic wrap and set aside at room temperature until needed.

MAKE THE MANDARIN ORANGE BASMATI RICE

Heat the peanut oil in a 3-quart saucepan over medium-high heat. When the oil is hot, add the rice and stir to coat with the oil. Season with salt and pepper, and stir to combine. Add the hot vegetable stock and rice wine, and stir to blend. Raise the heat to high and bring to a boil. As soon as the stock boils, cover the saucepan and lower the heat to medium. Continue to cook the rice until tender, about 15 minutes. Remove the rice from the heat and transfer to a 5-quart stainless steel bowl. Vigorously whisk the vinaigrette, then add ¼ cup to the rice. (Cover the remaining cup of vinaigrette with plastic wrap and set aside at room temperature until needed.) Use a rubber spatula to stir the ingredients, then add the mandarin orange sections and stir to combine. Adjust the seasoning. Set the rice aside, uncovered, for up to 2 hours at room temperature. Or cool to room temperature and then refrigerate in a covered, noncorrosive container for up to 24 hours before serving.

PREPARE THE SESAME STIR-FRIED VEGETABLES

Preheat the oven to 325 degrees Fahrenheit.

Toast the sesame seeds on a baking sheet in the preheated oven for 20 minutes, until golden brown. Remove from the oven and set aside to cool at room temperature until needed.

Heat 3 quarts of salted water in a 5-quart saucepan over medium-high heat until boiling. Add the snow peas and blanch for about 1 minute, until tender but still very crisp. Drain the snow peas in a colander, then immediately plunge them into ice water to stop the cooking and keep them bright green. Remove from the ice water and drain thoroughly.

Heat the peanut oil and sesame oil in a large nonstick sauté pan or in a wok over high heat. When the oil is hot, add the scallions and stir-fry for 30 seconds. Add the bok choy and water chestnuts, season with salt and pepper, and stir-fry for 2½ minutes. Add the snow peas and stir-fry for 1½ minutes. Add the toasted sesame seeds and toss to combine. Remove from the heat and set aside at room temperature while assembling the salad plates.

ASSEMBLE THE SALAD

Divide and arrange the Boston lettuce leaves on four 10- to 12-inch room-temperature plates. Vigorously whisk the vinaigrette. Dress each portion of lettuce with 1 to 1½ tablespoons of vinaigrette. Remove the tangy red cabbage from the refrigerator and stir to combine. Place an equal amount of the cabbage in a ring near the outside edge of the Boston lettuce on each plate. Place an equal amount of rice within each ring of cabbage.

Use a rubber spatula or a kitchen spoon to form a well 2 to 2½ inches in diameter in the center of the rice. Place an equal amount of stir-fried vegetables in the well in the center of the rice. Whisk the vinaigrette once again and dress the vegetables and rice with 2 to 2½ tablespoons of vinaigrette. Serve immediately.

※

*O*range and Cilantro Barbecued Catfish Variation

1 cup orange juice
¼ cup rice wine
¼ cup rice wine vinegar
2 tablespoons finely minced orange zest

1 tablespoon minced fresh cilantro
4 4-ounce skinless farm-raised catfish fillets
salt and freshly ground black pepper to taste

Heat the orange juice, rice wine, rice wine vinegar, and orange zest in a 1½-quart saucepan over high heat. Bring to a boil. Continue to boil for 15 minutes, until slightly thickened. Remove from the heat and transfer to a 3-quart stainless steel bowl. Cool in an ice and water bath to a temperature of 40 to 45 degrees Fahrenheit. When cool, add the cilantro and stir to combine. The orange-cilantro basting sauce may be used immediately or refrigerated in a covered noncorrosive container for a couple of days.

Season the catfish fillets with salt and pepper.

Grill the catfish over a medium wood or charcoal fire for 2 minutes, then turn and begin basting with the orange-cilantro basting sauce. Continue to grill and baste the fillets, turning as necessary, for 4 to 5 more minutes. Remove from the grill and place a fillet on top of each salad. Serve immediately.

※

*C*harred Flank Steak Variation

1 tablespoon Szechuan peppercorns
2 tablespoons soy sauce
2 tablespoons granulated sugar

¼ cup peanut oil
1 pound flank steak

Preheat the oven to 325 degrees Fahrenheit.

Toast the peppercorns in a pie tin in the preheated oven for 5 minutes. Cool the peppercorns to room temperature before finely grinding them in a spice or coffee grinder.

In a 3-quart stainless steel bowl, whisk together the soy sauce and sugar until the sugar has dissolved. Add the peanut oil in a slow, steady stream while whisking until emulsified and thick. Add the ground peppercorns and whisk to combine. Add the flank steak and turn a few times to coat with the marinade. Cover the bowl with plastic wrap and refrigerate for at least 2 hours (and up to 24 hours).

Heat a large nonstick sauté pan over high heat. When the pan is hot, place the flank steak in the pan and cook for 3 minutes on each side for rare meat. For medium-cooked meat, transfer the flank steak to a baking sheet and place in a 325-degree-Fahrenheit oven for 10 minutes. Slice the steak into thin slices across the grain. Place an equal amount on each salad. Serve immediately.

The Chef's Touch

THE HARVEST season in wine country is an emotional time when anticipation, anxiety, hope, joy, disappointment, and celebration all vie for the wine maker's psyche. It is also a frenetic time, so I was surprised that Jack and Dolores Cakebread, owners of Cakebread Cellars in Napa Valley, annually invited chefs and cottage industry food producers to their vineyard to participate in a hands-on forum during harvest. I was a delighted participant during the Third Annual American Harvest Workshop at Cakebread in September 1989 when our mission was to exchange ideas about food and wine pairings, and to promote the utilization of specialty foods. During the three days of the program, we toured local specialty food producers and returned daily to the Cakebread winery kitchen to prepare the bounty of Napa Valley. Besides our day's "catch," the kitchen pantry was always well stocked with everyday staples plus exotic grains, pastas, oils, and spices. I was not familiar with some items, including three uncommon rices: Black Thai, sweet Wehani, and basmati. I became so fond of the basmati rice that it is now a staple in The Trellis kitchen pantry.

Because basmati rice is aged for a year, it has an exceptional nutty flavor and a low moisture content that keeps the cooked rice firm and separated. Look for basmati rice in the specialty or bulk foods department at your grocery or in Middle Eastern or Indian markets (it is grown in Iran, India, and Pakistan).

Szechuan (or Sichuan) peppercorns have an extraordinary bosky and herbal

The Chef's Touch

flavor rather than a traditional peppery flavor. These strange-looking peppercorns (almost clovelike) provide some heat and an abundance of interesting flavor. We have used Szechuan peppercorns for more than seventeen years at The Trellis, and in fact they are the secret ingredient in our skirt steak marinade.

You may need to venture to an Asian market to find Szechuan peppercorns. Store them in a tightly sealed plastic container.

The Szechuan Vinaigrette recipe yields about 1¼ cups. You can keep the vinaigrette at room temperature for several hours before using or refrigerate it in a covered, noncorrosive container for 2 to 3 days. If refrigerated, return the vinaigrette to room temperature and whisk vigorously before using.

For this particular recipe we used canned Mandarin oranges. I like the way they break into sweet orange confetti when stirred into the still warm basmati rice. You may, of course, substitute an equal amount of fresh tangerines or clementines. One 11-ounce can of Mandarin oranges will yield 1 cup of drained orange sections.

We almost always find bok choy at the local market, which is good news because I am fond of its crunchy texture and mild cabbage flavor (exclusive of the green leaves). Select bok choy with blemish-free bright-green leaves.

Peeling fresh water chestnuts with a paring knife is not my idea of fun, but it's worth the effort. The nutty texture and pure flavor contrasts greatly with the porous, metallic-tasting canned variety.

One large head of Boston lettuce, about ¾ pound to 1 pound as purchased, should yield ½ pound of prepared lettuce. For crisp greens, spin-dry the washed leaves in a salad spinner.

Earlier in The Chef's Touch I mentioned that Szechuan peppercorns were the secret to The Trellis's skirt steak marinade. I should tell you that the flank steak variation marinade is not the same as the one we use at the restaurant for skirt steak. You will have to wait for my next book to get that highly sought after and never told recipe. Commonly known as London broil, flank steak is best eaten rare to medium-rare and thinly sliced.

I could be persuaded to accompany this salad with a young, softly fragrant red wine, uncomplicated but fairly expressive of fruit. From The Trellis wine list, that selection would be the Carneros Fleur de Pinot Noir from the Carneros Creek winery in the Carneros district of Napa Valley.

Penne Pasta and Spinach with Oven-Roasted Plum Tomatoes, Toasted Walnuts, Curly Endive, and Cracked Black Pepper Vinaigrette

Serves 4

Oven-Roasted Plum Tomatoes

12 medium plum tomatoes (about 2 ounces each), washed and cored

salt and freshly ground black pepper to taste

Cracked Black Pepper Vinaigrette

4 tablespoons cider vinegar
4 tablespoons fresh lemon juice
2 teaspoons freshly cracked black peppercorns

1 teaspoon salt
¾ cup extra-virgin olive oil

Pasta

1 pound penne pasta
Cracked Black Pepper Vinaigrette
¾ pound flat-leaf spinach, stemmed, cut widthwise into strips ½ inch wide, washed, and dried

salt and freshly ground black pepper to taste

Salad Greens and Garnish

1 cup walnuts
¾ pound curly endive, cored, trimmed, cut into ¾-inch pieces, washed, and dried

❧

ROAST THE PLUM TOMATOES

Preheat the oven to 225 degrees Fahrenheit.

Cut each plum tomato in half lengthwise, then cut each half into 2 sections lengthwise. Place the tomato sections, evenly spaced, and skin side down, on a baking sheet lined with parchment paper. Season lightly with salt and pepper. Place the tomatoes in the preheated oven and roast for 3 hours. Remove from the oven and cool to room temperature. The tomatoes can be kept at room temperature for 3 to 4 hours, until ready to use, or stored in a tightly sealed plastic container in the refrigerator for several days.

MAKE THE CRACKED BLACK PEPPER VINAIGRETTE

In a 3-quart stainless steel bowl, whisk together the cider vinegar, lemon juice, peppercorns, and salt. Add the olive oil in a slow, steady stream while whisking to incorporate. Cover with plastic wrap and set aside at room temperature while cooking the pasta.

PREPARE THE PASTA

Bring 3 quarts of salted water to a boil in a 5-quart saucepan over high heat. When boiling, add the penne pasta and cook, stirring frequently, about 12 minutes, until tender but firm to the bite. Thoroughly drain the pasta in a colander, then transfer to a 7-quart stainless steel bowl. Vigorously whisk the vinaigrette, then add ¾ cup to the pasta and toss to coat. (Cover the remaining ½ cup of vinaigrette with plastic wrap and set aside at room temperature until needed.)

Add the spinach, generously season with salt and pepper, and use a rubber spatula to combine. Set aside at room temperature, loosely covered with plastic wrap, for up to 2 hours before serving.

Equipment

paring knife
measuring spoons
measuring cup
salad spinner
cook's knife
cutting board
baking sheet
parchment paper
3-quart stainless steel bowl
whisk
plastic wrap
5-quart saucepan
colander
7-quart stainless steel bowl
rubber spatula

Chicken variation requires:
aluminum foil
meat cleaver
charcoal grill
tongs

Salmon variation requires:
large nonstick sauté pan
spatula

FINISH AND ASSEMBLE THE SALAD

Preheat the oven to 325 degrees Fahrenheit.

Toast the walnuts on a baking sheet in the preheated oven for 10 minutes. Set aside.

Divide and arrange the curly endive on four 10- to 12-inch room-temperature soup or pasta plates. Vigorously whisk the vinaigrette. Dress the curly endive with 2 tablespoons of vinaigrette. Place equal amounts of pasta on each portion of endive. Randomly place 12 oven-roasted tomato sections on each portion of pasta. Sprinkle the walnuts on each salad. Serve immediately.

❧

Grilled Chicken Breast Variation

4 4-ounce boneless, skinless chicken breasts

2 tablespoons fresh lemon juice

2 tablespoons sauvignon blanc or other dry
  white wine

salt and freshly ground black pepper to taste

1 teaspoon vegetable oil

Trim any excess fat from the chicken breasts. Sprinkle the lemon juice and white wine on both sides of the breasts, then season each side with salt and pepper. Place the chicken breasts, one at a time, between 2 sheets of lightly oiled aluminum foil or parchment paper. Slightly flatten each breast using a meat cleaver or the bottom of a heavy-duty sauté pan. Cook immediately or cover each chicken breast with plastic wrap and refrigerate until ready to use (up to 24 hours).

Grill the chicken breasts over a medium wood or charcoal fire for 2½ to 3 minutes on each side. (The chicken breasts may also be pan-seared in a large, lightly oiled, nonstick sauté pan over medium heat. Cook for about the same amount of time as for grilling.) Place a chicken breast on each salad. Serve immediately.

*P*an-Seared Salmon Variation

3 tablespoons fresh lemon juice
1 tablespoon extra-virgin olive oil

salt and freshly ground black pepper to taste
4 4- to 5-ounce skinless salmon fillets

Sprinkle the lemon juice, olive oil, salt, and pepper on both sides of the salmon fillets. Cook immediately or cover each fillet with plastic wrap and refrigerate until needed (up to 24 hours).

Heat a large nonstick sauté pan over medium-high heat. When the pan is hot, place the salmon fillets in the pan and cook for 1½ to 2 minutes on each side for medium-rare—or longer if you prefer the salmon cooked through. Place a cooked salmon fillet on each salad. Serve immediately.

The Chef's Touch

WHEN I invited my friend Jim Seu to join us for lunch at Ganache Hill during the recipe testing phase of this book, I wanted to prepare a salad that was distinctly Italian. Jim had just retired after operating his own restaurant for forty-two years. During those years he had acquired innumerable friends from all walks of life, including a small group of fellow Italian Americans (and occasionally some honorary Italians) that gathered once a month for an Italian-inspired luncheon at Jim's Colonial Restaurant. Now that his retirement had eliminated those cherished gatherings, I invited Jim and his *paesani* to be taste testers and made a luncheon–cum–retirement party out of the occasion. Animated conversation, good wine, and this penne salad were deemed delicious by all, including Jim's friend Mimmo, who was visiting from Italy.

Oven-roasted tomatoes taste as sweet as candy, no matter the time of year. The process is simple, albeit time-consuming. My suggestion is to pop them in the oven and then plug *The Godfather* into your VCR. When the film is over (part one is 175 minutes long), it's time to remove the tomatoes from the oven.

(continued on next page)

Other types, from cherry tomatoes to beefsteak tomatoes, can be oven-roasted. The flavor of each is drastically improved by the slow oven-roasting process, especially during the nine or ten months of the year when sweet, ripe, fresh tomatoes are hard to come by.

The Black Pepper Vinaigrette recipe yields about 1¼ cups. The vinaigrette may be kept at room temperature for several hours before using or refrigerated in a covered, noncorrosive container for 2 to 3 days. If refrigerated, return the vinaigrette to room temperature and whisk vigorously before using.

Although I have tasted many imported box pastas, none measures up to De Cecco Pasta. This is the dried pasta that we have used at The Trellis for seventeen years, and it's the brand that is worth the search. (Jim's friend Mimmo averred that De Cecco was also considered one of the best by Italians.)

One large bunch of flat-leaf spinach, about ¾ pound as purchased, should yield ½ pound of stemmed leaves. For crisp greens, spin-dry the washed spinach leaves in a salad spinner.

One medium head of curly endive, about ¾ pound as purchased, should yield ½ pound of prepared greens. For crisp greens, spin-dry the washed curly endive pieces in a salad spinner.

I love pasta, so I find the portion of this salad just right. If it looks like too much to you, then invite a couple of extra friends over—as long as they bring the wine.

Since this is far from being a pretentious salad, I have intentionally kept the variations straightforward: Grilled Chicken Breast or Pan-Seared Salmon. If you feel compelled to "jazz up" the variations, consider seasoning with a spice. A light dusting of one of the following just prior to cooking is certain to give it a slightly different flavor identity: Hungarian paprika, curry powder, cayenne pepper, or even cinnamon.

Rather than taking the easy way out and selecting an Italian wine to accompany this salad for our luncheon, I had some fun and offered a red California zinfandel wine. Although the origin of the zinfandel grape is Italian, many think it is indigenous to California. Regardless, it can be made into some distinctly different-style wines. I chose a Kenwood, Nuns Canyon, Zinfandel, which is full of life and has a fruity or raspberry quality.

Marinated Cauliflower, Celery, and Red Onion, with Watercress, Quinoa, and Herbed Yogurt Dressing

Serves 4

Herbed Yogurt Dressing

1 cup plain lowfat yogurt
2 tablespoons fresh lemon juice
2 tablespoons chopped fresh Italian parsley

1 tablespoon chopped fresh dill
1 tablespoon chopped fresh mint
salt and freshly ground black pepper to taste

Marinated Cauliflower, Celery, and Red Onion

1 large head white cauliflower (about
   2 pounds), trimmed, cored, cut into small
   florets, sliced ¼ inch thick, washed, and
   drained
4 stalks celery (about ½ pound), trimmed,
   washed, and cut diagonally into strips
   2 inches long and ¼ inch thick
1 large red onion (about ½ pound), peeled
   and thinly sliced

2 cups dry white wine
½ cup white wine vinegar
4 cloves garlic, peeled
1 lemon, cut into ½-inch pieces, seeds
   removed
1 tablespoon whole black peppercorns
1 medium bay leaf
½ cup extra-virgin olive oil
salt and freshly ground black pepper to taste

Quinoa

2 cups quinoa
4 cups Vegetable Stock (see page 26)
1 teaspoon salt

3 tablespoons extra-virgin olive oil
freshly ground black pepper to taste

Salad Greens

½ pound watercress, trimmed, washed, and
   dried

Equipment

measuring cup
measuring spoons
cook's knife
cutting board
paring knife
colander
salad spinner
3-quart stainless steel bowl
whisk
plastic wrap
5-quart saucepan
3-quart saucepan with lid
medium-gauge strainer
7-quart stainless steel bowl
rubber spatula
baking sheet
5-quart stainless steel bowl
slotted spoon

*Mahi mahi variation
  requires:*
basting brush
charcoal grill
spatula

Pheasant variation requires:
aluminum foil
meat cleaver
smoker
parchment paper

MAKE THE HERBED YOGURT DRESSING

In a 3-quart stainless steel bowl, whisk together the yogurt, lemon juice, parsley, dill, and mint until thoroughly combined. Season with salt and pepper. Cover tightly with plastic wrap and refrigerate until needed.

PREPARE THE MARINATED VEGETABLES

Place the sliced cauliflower, celery, and red onion in a 5-quart saucepan. Set aside.

Heat the white wine, white wine vinegar, garlic, lemon pieces, peppercorns, and bay leaf in a 3-quart saucepan over medium-high heat. Bring the marinade to a boil, then adjust the heat and simmer for 10 minutes. Strain the marinade and pour over the vegetables in the 5-quart saucepan. Heat the vegetables in the marinade over medium-high heat. As soon as the marinade begins to boil, remove from the heat and transfer the vegetables along with the marinade to a 7-quart stainless steel bowl. Add the olive oil and use a rubber spatula to combine. Season with salt and pepper. Immediately cover tightly with plastic wrap and refrigerate for at least 1 hour before serving. (The marinated vegetables may be refrigerated for 2 to 3 days in a covered, noncorrosive container.)

PREPARE THE QUINOA

Preheat the oven to 325 degrees Fahrenheit.

Place the quinoa in a medium-gauge strainer and rinse thoroughly with cold water.

Toast the quinoa on a baking sheet in the preheated oven for 15 minutes to bring out the unique nutty flavor of the quinoa.

Heat the vegetable stock with 1 teaspoon of salt in a 3-quart saucepan over medium-high heat. Bring to a boil. Add the quinoa and return to a boil. Turn the heat to medium-low and simmer, covered, for 15 minutes, until most of the liquid has evaporated. Transfer the quinoa to a 5-quart stainless steel bowl. Add the olive oil and use a rubber spatula to combine. Season with salt and pepper. Cool, uncovered, at room temperature for 1 hour, stirring occasionally.

ASSEMBLE THE SALAD

Divide and arrange the watercress in a ring, stem ends toward the center, with the leaf ends near the outside edge of four 10- to 12-inch room-temperature soup or pasta plates. Place an equal amount of quinoa (about 1½ cups) in a ring inside the ring of watercress. Use a slotted spoon to place an equal amount of marinated cauliflower in the center of the quinoa ring. Sprinkle each salad with 3 to 4 tablespoons of dressing. Serve immediately.

$

Grilled Mahi Mahi with Lemon and Dill Variation

2 tablespoons fresh lemon juice

4 4- to 5-ounce skinless mahi mahi fillets

salt and freshly ground black pepper to taste

2 tablespoons extra-virgin olive oil

1 lemon, peeled and sectioned

1 tablespoon chopped fresh dill

Sprinkle the lemon juice over both sides of the mahi mahi fillets, then lightly season each side with salt and pepper. Cook immediately or cover each fillet with plastic wrap and refrigerate until needed (up to 24 hours).

Brush the mahi mahi fillets on both sides with the olive oil. Grill the fillets over a medium wood or charcoal fire until done, about 4½ minutes on each side. (The mahi mahi fillets may also be pan-seared in a large, lightly oiled nonstick sauté pan over medium-high heat. Cook for about the same amount of time as listed for grilling.) Place a mahi mahi fillet on each salad, garnish with lemon sections and chopped dill, and serve immediately.

Smoked Pheasant Breast Variation

4 5- to 6-ounce boneless, skinless pheasant   ½ cup kosher salt
  breasts   ½ cup honey
1 teaspoon vegetable oil   ½ cup cool water
1 cup warm water

Trim any excess fat, skin, and membrane from the pheasant breasts. Place the breasts, one at a time, between 2 sheets of lightly oiled aluminum foil or parchment paper. Slightly flatten each breast using a meat cleaver or the bottom of a heavy-duty sauté pan.

Prepare a brine in a 3-quart stainless steel bowl by combining the warm water, kosher salt, and ¼ cup of honey. Whisk to dissolve the salt and honey. Add the cool water and stir to combine. Immerse the pheasant breasts in the brine for 5 minutes, turning the breasts over halfway through the immersion time. Remove the breasts from the brine and transfer to a baking sheet lined with plastic wrap. Place the pheasant, uncovered, in the refrigerator for 30 minutes.

Line the top wire shelf of a smoker with parchment paper. Place the breasts on the shelf in the smoker and smoke for 2 hours.

Preheat the oven to 350 degrees Fahrenheit.

Remove the breasts with the parchment paper from the smoker and transfer to a baking sheet. Coat both sides of each of the 4 breasts with the remaining ¼ cup of honey. Return the breasts to the parchment paper on the baking sheet. Place in the preheated oven to cook for 15 minutes. Remove the breasts from the oven and cool to room temperature. Transfer the breasts to a cutting board and cut each diagonally into slices 3 inches long and ¼ inch thick. Arrange 1 sliced breast onto each salad. Serve immediately.

The Chef's Touch

QUINOA DATES back to the ancient Incas, but now this "hot, new" grain is achieving notoriety in the U.S.A. because of its uniquely nutty and delicious flavor.

I first encountered quinoa in 1992 at a General Foods Nutrition scholarship class at The Culinary Institute of America. My fellow classmates and I prepared herbed quinoa and red lentils as an accompaniment to poached salmon wrapped in savoy cabbage leaves. This dish scored high in presentation, taste, and texture.

In Williamsburg I found quinoa in a health food store (it is also available in the bulk foods section at most major supermarkets). Uncooked quinoa should be stored at room temperature in a tightly sealed plastic container. Before using, be sure to rinse the tiny ivory quinoa beads thoroughly, since they may be coated with saponin, a natural plant substance good for producing foam in beverages and detergents but bad for fresh salads. Also, make sure you toast the quinoa *after* rinsing to enhance the sweet, nutty flavor of the grain.

A ratio of 1 cup of quinoa to 2 cups of stock produces 3 cups of cooked quinoa. I have seen recipes that claim this grain expands to four times its original volume. Not so in my kitchen.

The Herbed Yogurt Dressing recipe yields 1¼ cups. The dressing may be stored tightly covered in the refrigerator for 3 or 4 days.

Although this recipe calls for readily available white cauliflower, some of the colorful hybrids or the fluorescent green broccoflower (you guessed it, a cross between broccoli and cauliflower) are delightful substitutes. Don't purchase cauliflower with brown blemishes or an overly vegetal aroma, and use it within two to three days of purchase.

If you prefer, you may use chicken stock rather than vegetable stock to prepare the quinoa, giving the cooked grains a slightly richer flavor. You can also substitute smoked duck or chicken for the pheasant.

One large bunch of watercress, about ½ pound as purchased, should yield ¼ pound of trimmed (cut away about ½ inch of the stem ends), washed, and dried leaves. For crisp greens, spin-dry the watercress in a salad spinner. Watercress is very perishable, so make certain you purchase it very fresh, and select only

(*continued on next page*)

those bunches that have brightly colored green leaves. When selecting watercress, pick it up and smell it, and don't purchase it if the watercress has a strong vegetal smell. Store the watercress stem ends covered with ice in the refrigerator, and use within a day or two.

Mahi mahi is a delicious fin fish (at The Trellis we call it by its proper name, dolphin—not to be confused with the mammal of the same name). Due to its fairly high fat content, it is an excellent candidate for grilling.

The firm texture of mahi mahi allows for placing the cooked fish in a preheated 200-degree-Fahrenheit oven to keep warm for 15 to 20 minutes after grilling or pan-searing. Don't garnish the fish with the lemon sections and dill until the cooked fish portions are placed on the salads.

American-crafted pinot noir wines have come into their own during the last few years. I remember when they were routinely judged as inferior to red burgundies made with the same grape. Today some remarkable pinot noirs are being produced in California as well as in Oregon and Washington State. A youthful American pinot noir with ripe fruit flavor would work well with this salad and either one of the variations.

Arborio Rice Cakes with Marinated Plum Tomatoes, Artichokes, and Sweet Peppers on a Bed of Leaf Spinach with Saffron Vinaigrette

Serves 4

Arborio Rice Cakes

1 tablespoon extra-virgin olive oil
½ cup finely minced onion
1 cup arborio rice
½ cup sauvignon blanc or other dry white wine

2½ cups hot saffron-infused vegetable stock (see page 140)
salt and freshly ground black pepper to taste

Marinated Plum Tomatoes, Artichokes, and Sweet Peppers

4 medium artichokes (about 8 to 10 ounces each)
1 tablespoon plus 1 teaspoon fresh lemon juice
8 medium plum tomatoes (about 2 ounces each), washed, cored, and cut into ¼-inch cubes
2 large red bell peppers (about 1 pound), roasted, skinned, seeded, and cut into ¼-inch-wide strips the length of the pepper

2 large yellow bell peppers (about 1 pound), roasted, skinned, seeded, and cut into ¼-inch-wide strips the length of the pepper
2 tablespoons extra-virgin olive oil
1 tablespoon balsamic vinegar
salt and freshly ground black pepper to taste
¼ cup chopped fresh basil

Equipment

measuring cup
1½-quart saucepan
measuring spoons
paring knife
cook's knife
cutting board
3-quart saucepan
salad spinner
two 3-quart stainless steel
   bowls
whisk
plastic wrap
wooden kitchen spoon
10- by 15-inch nonstick
   baking sheet with sides
rubber spatula
5-quart saucepan
stainless steel cook's knife
sharp-edged spoon
metal skewer
colander
7-quart stainless steel bowl
metal spatula

Oyster variation requires:
pie tin
2 baking sheets
large nonstick sauté pan
tongs
paper towels

Beef variation requires:
pie tin
medium nonstick
   sauté pan
tongs
slicer

Salad Greens

¾ pound flat-leaf spinach, stemmed, washed, and dried

Saffron Vinaigrette

¼ cup Saffron-Infused White Wine Vinegar (see page 25)
¼ cup extra-virgin olive oil
¼ cup safflower oil
salt and freshly ground black pepper to taste

ꝝ

MAKE THE SAFFRON VINAIGRETTE
Place the saffron-infused white wine vinegar in a 3-quart
stainless steel bowl. Add the olive oil in a slow, steady stream
while whisking until incorporated. Add the safflower oil and
whisk to combine fully. Season with salt and pepper and whisk
to combine. Cover tightly with plastic wrap and set aside at
room temperature until needed.

PREPARE THE RICE CAKE MIXTURE
Heat the olive oil in a 3-quart saucepan over medium heat.
When hot, add the onions and cook, stirring frequently, until
the onions are tender, about 2 minutes. Add the rice and stir to
combine with the onions. Add the white wine and cook, stirring
constantly, until the wine is absorbed, about 2 minutes. Add 1
cup of hot stock and continue to cook the rice, constantly stirring, until the stock is absorbed, about 4 minutes. Add 1 more
cup of hot stock and cook, once again stirring constantly, until
the stock is absorbed, about 6 minutes. Add the remaining ½
cup of hot stock and cook, stirring constantly, until the rice is
thick and creamy, about 5 minutes. Season with salt and pepper. (Be certain to taste the rice mixture and season as needed.)
Pour the rice mixture in a 10- by 15-inch nonstick baking sheet
with sides, using a rubber spatula to spread the mixture over
half of the sheet to a uniform thickness. (The thickness of the
mixture will prevent it from running over onto the other half

after it is spread out.) Refrigerate the rice mixture, uncovered, until thoroughly chilled, about 1 to 1½ hours.

MAKE THE MARINATED TOMATOES, ARTICHOKES, AND SWEET PEPPERS

In a 5-quart stainless steel or glass saucepan, bring 3 quarts of lightly salted water to a boil. While the water is heating, prepare the artichokes for cooking: Remove the outer leaves from the artichokes by grasping each leaf individually and pulling it away until it snaps off. Use a stainless steel knife to slice off the top third of the flower (the cone-shaped, pale green part of the artichoke that remains after the leaves have been removed). Using a sharp-edged spoon, scrape out the fuzzy thistle from the center of each artichoke. Cut away all but ¼ inch of each stem. Place the artichokes, as soon as you cut and trim each one, into 2 quarts of cold water mixed with 1 tablespoon of lemon juice. Keep the artichokes in the acidulated water for no more than a few minutes, then drain and add to the salted boiling water. (If the artichokes remain in the acidulated water for very long, they will pick up an overly acidic flavor.) Cook the artichokes in the boiling water until cooked through, about 20 to 25 minutes. They are done when easily pierced by a skewer. Drain the cooked artichokes in a colander and then immediately plunge into ice water (to prevent the artichokes from continuing to cook). Remove from the ice water and drain well. Peel the fibrous outer layer from the artichokes, cut each in half, and then slice lengthwise into pieces ¼ inch thick.

Place the artichoke pieces, tomatoes, and red and yellow bell pepper strips into a 7-quart stainless steel bowl. Sprinkle the olive oil, vinegar, and the remaining 1 teaspoon of lemon juice over the vegetables. Season with salt and pepper. Use a rubber spatula to stir and combine the vegetables. Cover with plastic wrap and set aside at room temperature while cooking the rice cakes. (The basil will be added just before serving.)

COOK THE RICE CAKES

Preheat the oven to 350 degrees Fahrenheit.

Remove the rice cake mixture from the refrigerator. Turn the baking sheet over onto a clean, dry cutting board and lift the baking sheet off the inverted rice mixture. Cut the solidified rice cake mixture in half lengthwise, then cut each half lengthwise in half. Make 3 cuts widthwise to make equal fourths, giving you 16 portions. Use a metal spatula to place the cakes, evenly spaced, on a clean, dry nonstick baking sheet. Place the baking sheet in the preheated oven and bake the cakes until slightly crispy on the outside but deliciously moist and tender on the inside, about 20 to 25 minutes. The cakes can be served immediately or kept in a 200-degree-Fahrenheit oven for up to 30 minutes.

FINISH AND ASSEMBLE THE SALAD

Add the basil to the marinated vegetables and stir with a rubber spatula to combine.

Divide and arrange the spinach leaves on four 10- to 12-inch room-temperature plates. Vigorously whisk the vinaigrette and dress each salad with 2 to 3 tablespoons of vinaigrette. Place an equal amount (about 1 cup) of the marinated vegetable mixture onto the center of each bed of spinach. Place 4 hot and crispy rice cakes on each salad, around the vegetables. Serve immediately.

*P*anfried Oysters Variation

1 cup yellow cornmeal

1 teaspoon salt

1/8 teaspoon ground cayenne pepper

1 pint shucked oysters, drained

1 cup safflower oil

Preheat the oven to 200 degrees Fahrenheit.

Combine the cornmeal, salt, and cayenne pepper together in a pie tin or similar-size shallow dish.

Place a few oysters at a time in the cornmeal mixture. (If you try to do them all at once, the oysters will not get evenly coated.) Gently toss to coat the oysters evenly and lightly with the cornmeal. Transfer the coated oysters to a baking sheet or platter; repeat until all the oysters are coated.

Heat 1/2 cup of safflower oil in a large nonstick sauté pan over medium-high heat. When the oil is very hot, panfry half of the oysters for 30 to 45 seconds on each side, until golden brown and crispy. Remove the oysters from the pan and transfer to a baking sheet lined with paper towels. Place the baking sheet in the preheated oven to keep the oysters warm while frying the second batch. Wipe the sauté pan clean, then heat the remaining 1/2 cup of safflower oil until very hot. Repeat the panfrying process with the remaining oysters. Transfer the fried oysters to the baking sheet lined with paper towels to drain for a few seconds. Divide the oysters among the salads and serve immediately.

ɮ

Charred Raw Tenderloin of Beef Variation

1 pound well-trimmed beef tenderloin
2 tablespoons extra-virgin olive oil
salt to taste

3 tablespoons freshly cracked black
  peppercorns

Place the beef tenderloin in a pie tin or similar-size shallow dish that contains the olive oil. Coat the meat evenly with the oil. Season the tenderloin with salt, then sprinkle the peppercorns on the meat, covering as much of the surface area as possible. Use your hands to press the peppercorns into the meat.

Heat a medium nonstick sauté pan over high heat until smoking hot. Place the tenderloin in the pan and char evenly by turning frequently for 3 to 4 minutes. Remove the tenderloin from the pan and transfer to a dish or plate large enough to hold it. Refrigerate the tenderloin for 1½ to 2 hours, until thoroughly chilled.

Place the tenderloin on a cutting board and use a very sharp slicer to cut the meat into very thin slices (about 16 to 20 slices). Divide the slices among the salads. Serve immediately.

The Chef's Touch

I LIKE this salad so much that when I wrote this book in the winter of 1997, I decided to prepare it at a class I would teach the following spring at La Varenne at the Greenbrier in White Sulphur Springs, West Virginia. The venerable Greenbrier resort was celebrating twenty years of world-class cooking programs, and although this was my tenth teaching appearance at the Greenbrier in as many years, I felt challenged by the significance of the anniversary to put together a class that would impart visual as well as taste memories. This salad certainly does that.

The Saffron Vinaigrette recipe yields ¾ cup. The vinaigrette may be kept

(continued on next page)

at room temperature for several hours before using or refrigerated in a covered, noncorrosive container for several days. If refrigerated, return the dressing to room temperature and whisk vigorously before using.

The short stubby grains that give arborio rice its distinctive appearance offer no indication of the high starch content of this Italian-grown rice. The starch, along with the slow cooking and constant stirring, produces the creamy texture and fools the palate into thinking that cream or cheese must be in the cooked rice. And remember, there is no substitute for arborio rice or the constant stirring.

To prepare the saffron-infused vegetable stock (see page 26 for the Vegetable Stock recipe), heat 2½ cups of vegetable stock to a simmer in a 3-quart saucepan over medium-high heat. Remove the stock from the heat as soon as it begins to simmer and add 2 small pinches of saffron (about 1 gram). Steep the saffron in the stock for 1 hour before using. This step can be done a few hours or even a day or so before preparing the arborio rice cakes. For extended storage, keep the infused stock covered in the refrigerator until ready to use.

If common artichokes are not available or you find their preparation too daunting, consider replacing them with cooked cauliflower florets or even raw strips of seeded cucumber.

The clean, herbal flavor of fresh basil cannot be replaced by dried basil. If fresh basil is not available, use another fresh herb such as parsley—more for color than flavor—or eliminate the herb altogether.

You may want to use the more readily available green bell pepper if other colored sweet peppers are not available.

One large bunch of flat-leaf spinach, about ¾ pound as purchased, should yield ½ pound of stemmed leaves. If flat-leaf spinach is not available, use an equal amount of stemmed, washed, and dried curly spinach. For crisp greens, spin-dry the washed spinach in a salad spinner.

For great-looking panfried oysters, place the cornmeal-coated oysters in the hot oil one at a time rather than attempting to put in a handful. You need to move quickly when doing this; otherwise, some of the oysters will be done before you put the last oysters in the pan. You will be rewarded for your celerity with some beautifully fried, seemingly greaseless oysters.

The Chef's Touch

After the charred beef tenderloin is completely chilled, you can keep it in the refrigerator, tightly covered with plastic wrap, for 1 or 2 days before serving.

The Viognier grape seems to be in vogue in the United States. Although some wine makers craft a somewhat thin Viognier wine, this is not the case with Horton Vineyard Viognier from Virginia. I like the sassiness of this spicy wine and the way it holds its own with this hearty salad.

*P*eppered Wild Rice with Honey-Bourbon Yams, Assorted Salad Greens, and Red Grape and Thyme Vinaigrette

Serves 4

Red Grape and Thyme Vinaigrette

³⁄₄ cup safflower oil
2 tablespoons cider vinegar
2 tablespoons sherry wine
  vinegar
½ pound red seedless grapes, stemmed,
  washed, and cut in quarters
1 tablespoon chopped fresh thyme
salt and freshly ground black pepper to taste

Peppered Wild Rice

2 cups Vegetable Stock (see page 26)
1 cup wild rice
salt and freshly ground black pepper to taste
1 tablespoon safflower oil
1 cup finely chopped onion
½ cup finely chopped green bell pepper
½ cup finely chopped red bell pepper
½ cup finely chopped celery
2 teaspoons freshly cracked black
  peppercorns
Red Grape and Thyme Vinaigrette

Honey-Bourbon Yams

3 medium yams or sweet potatoes (about
  2 pounds), unpeeled
salt and freshly ground black pepper
½ cup honey
2 tablespoons bourbon

Salad Greens and Garnish

½ pound curly endive, cored, trimmed,
  washed, and dried
½ pound flat-leaf spinach or curly spinach,
  stemmed, washed, and dried
½ pound watercress, trimmed, washed, and
  dried

MAKE THE RED GRAPE AND THYME VINAIGRETTE

In a 3-quart stainless steel bowl, vigorously whisk together the safflower oil, cider vinegar, and sherry wine vinegar. Add the red grapes and chopped thyme. Season with salt and pepper, and whisk to combine. Cover tightly with plastic wrap and set aside at room temperature until needed.

PREPARE THE PEPPERED WILD RICE

Heat the vegetable stock to a boil in a 3-quart saucepan over high heat.

Heat 2 inches of water in the bottom half of a double boiler over medium heat. With the heat on, add the boiling vegetable stock and wild rice to the top half of the double boiler. Season lightly with salt and pepper and cover tightly. Cook the rice over medium heat for about 1 hour, until cooked but slightly firm to the bite.

While the rice is cooking, heat the safflower oil in a medium nonstick sauté pan over medium-high heat. When the oil is hot, add the onion, green and red bell peppers, and celery, and sauté for 6 minutes, until tender. Remove from the heat and transfer to a 7-quart stainless steel bowl.

Drain the excess liquid from the cooked rice before adding the rice to the sautéed vegetables. Add the peppercorns and stir to combine. Vigorously whisk the vinaigrette, then add 1 cup to the wild rice and vegetables. (Cover the remaining ¾ cup of vinaigrette with plastic wrap and set aside at room temperature until needed.) Use a rubber spatula to combine the ingredients. Set the peppered wild rice aside at room temperature, loosely covered with plastic wrap, for up to 3 hours before serving. Or cool to room temperature and then refrigerate in a covered container for up to 2 days before serving.

PREPARE THE HONEY-BOURBON YAMS

Cook the whole yams in a 5-quart saucepan of boiling salted water for 35 minutes. Drain the cooking water from the yams.

Equipment

measuring cup
measuring spoons
cook's knife
cutting board
salad spinner
3-quart stainless steel bowl
whisk
plastic wrap
3-quart saucepan
double boiler
medium nonstick sauté pan
rubber spatula
two 7-quart stainless steel bowls
colander
5-quart saucepan
paring knife
2 large nonstick sauté pans
1-quart stainless steel bowl
spatula
2 nonstick baking sheets
basting brush

Duck variation requires:
paper towels
smoker
parchment paper

Lamb variation requires:
5-quart stainless steel bowl
large nonstick sauté pan

Cool the yams under cold running water for 5 minutes. Drain and refrigerate, uncovered, for 1 hour.

Preheat the oven to 200 degrees Fahrenheit.

Use a paring knife to peel and trim the ends from the cold yams. Slice the yams, slightly on the bias, into ¼-inch-thick slices (discard the ends). Season both sides of the yam slices with salt and pepper.

Heat 2 large nonstick sauté pans over medium-high heat. While the pans are getting hot, whisk together the honey and bourbon in a 1-quart stainless steel bowl. Dip the yam slices in the honey-bourbon mixture, then place them in the hot pans. Cook the yam slices for 1½ minutes on each side, until golden brown. Transfer the slices on 2 nonstick baking sheets. Lightly brush the top side of the yam slices with the remaining honey-bourbon mixture and place in the preheated oven until ready to serve, up to 30 minutes.

FINISH AND ASSEMBLE THE SALAD

Combine the curly endive, spinach, and watercress in a 7-quart stainless steel bowl. Vigorously whisk the remaining ¾ cup of vinaigrette. Add the vinaigrette to the greens and toss until the leaves are coated. (At first it may appear that this is not enough vinaigrette to thoroughly coat the greens; be assured that it is.) Divide and arrange the greens in a mound in the center of each of four 10- to 12-inch room-temperature plates. Spoon slightly more than 1 cup of peppered wild rice in a ring around each mound of greens. Place an equal amount of warm yam slices around each mound of greens. Serve immediately.

Smoked Duck and Dried Fruit Variation

¼ cup bourbon
¼ cup warm water
2 tablespoons honey
2 tablespoons kosher salt
¼ cup cool water

2 3-ounce boneless, skinless duck breasts
3 ounces dried peaches, cut in ¼-inch-wide
  strips the length of the peach
¼ cup dried currants
2 tablespoons crème de cassis

Prepare a brine in a 3-quart stainless steel bowl by combining the bourbon, warm water, honey, and kosher salt. Whisk to dissolve the honey and salt. Add the cool water and stir to combine. Immerse the duck breasts in the brine for 2 minutes, turning the breasts over halfway through the immersion time. Remove the breasts from the brine and pat dry with paper towels.

Line the top wire shelf of a smoker with parchment paper. Place the breasts on the shelf in the smoker and smoke for 2 hours.

Preheat the oven to 350 degrees Fahrenheit.

Remove the duck breasts (with the parchment paper) from the smoker and transfer to a baking sheet. Place the breasts in the preheated oven to cook for 10 minutes. Remove the breasts from the oven and cool at room temperature for 30 minutes.

Cut the duck into strips 3 inches long and 1/4 inch wide. Place the duck meat in a 3-quart stainless steel bowl. Add the peaches, currants, and cassis, and toss to combine. Place an equal amount of the mixture on each salad. Serve immediately. Or cool to room temperature and then refrigerate in a covered, noncorrosive container for up to 2 days before serving.

$$\approx$$

Caramelized Onion and Lamb Burger Variation

1 tablespoon safflower oil
1 medium onion (about 6 ounces), peeled
   and thinly sliced

salt and freshly ground black pepper to taste
1 teaspoon chopped fresh thyme
1 pound ground lamb from shoulder or leg

Heat the safflower oil in a medium nonstick sauté pan over medium heat. When the oil is hot, add the sliced onion and season lightly with salt and pepper. Cook the onion, stirring as necessary to prevent sticking and burning, for 20 minutes, until golden brown. Remove the onion from the heat, add the chopped thyme, and stir to combine. Transfer to a dish and place, uncovered, in the refrigerator to cool.

In a 5-quart stainless steel bowl, gently but thoroughly combine the ground lamb and chilled caramelized onion and thyme mixture.

Gently form the meat mixture into four 4-ounce burgers 1 inch thick. Cover with plastic wrap and refrigerate until needed (up to 24 hours).

Season the burgers with salt and pepper.

Heat a large nonstick sauté pan over medium-high heat. When hot, sear the burgers for 3 minutes on each side for a delicious medium-rare; cook longer on each side for more well done burgers. Place a burger on each salad. Serve immediately.

The Chef's Touch

W H E N I worked for the Colonial Williamsburg Foundation in the early 70s, my duties included searching out new food items for the Foundation's restaurants and taverns. Wild rice at that time was very expensive, and its use in Colonial Williamsburg–owned operations was therefore limited to a blend of wild rice and converted rice. Since wild rice takes longer to cook than converted rice, the end result was either undercooked wild rice or mushy converted rice. I related this problem to an Armenian restaurateur friend of mine in New York City who introduced me to a Swiss food broker who marketed Minnesota wild rice (go figure). After some negotiating, the broker agreed to sell the wild rice to the Foundation for less than what the Foundation paid for the wild rice blend. Consequently, wild rice purchases burgeoned in the restaurants and taverns, and the guests experienced a uniquely North American food in its pure form, many for the first time.

Take care not to undercook wild rice; the grains will be too hard and the flavor will not be developed. Likewise, don't overcook it, or the grains will be mushy and the nutty flavor considerably diminished. Perfectly cooked individual rice grains begin to split and appear variegated. Using the double boiler method as described in this recipe is about as close to foolproof cooking as it gets.

The Red Grape and Thyme Vinaigrette recipe yields 1¾ cups. The vinaigrette may be kept at room temperature for a couple of hours before using or refrigerated in a covered, noncorrosive container for up to 2 days. If refrigerated, return the vinaigrette to room temperature and whisk vigorously before using.

One small head of curly endive, about ½ pound as purchased, should yield ¼ pound prepared greens. A half pound of flat-leaf or curly spinach will yield ¼ pound of prepared leaves. One large bunch of watercress, about ½ pound as purchased, will yield ¼ pound of trimmed (cut away about ½ inch of the stem ends), washed, and dried leaves. For crisp greens, separately spin-dry the washed curly endive, spinach, and watercress in a salad spinner.

We use so much watercress year-round at The Trellis that I thought we might end up in the *Guinness Book of World Records* for our lavish usage of this slightly peppery but notably delicious green. No matter how much or how

The Chef's Touch

little you use, if you keep it refrigerated for more than a day, you will maintain the quality by keeping the stem ends iced. The delicate flavor of watercress deteriorates in a matter of a few days, and even your pet goat may reject it when it gets an overly grassy taste.

You can use sweet potatoes rather than yams for this recipe but look for similar-sized vegetables. (It's tempting to call them potatoes, but a true sweet potato is not a tuber, as are potatoes, but a root. And to make things even more interesting, a true yam is neither root nor tuber but actually a rhizome.) Select in the 10- to 12-ounce range. I make a point of this as yams can get rather large—would you believe 30 to 100 pounds?

Toasted pecans can add delicious crunch to this salad. Toast ½ cup of pecan halves on a baking sheet in a preheated 325-degree-Fahrenheit oven for 10 minutes. Cool to room temperature before using. Sprinkle a few pecans over each salad before serving.

You may be able to purchase duck breasts from your butcher. Otherwise, select a 4-pound dressed duck (which should yield two breasts each weighing about 3 ounces, slightly more or less) and do the deed yourself.

I like the sweetness that the crème de cassis adds to the smoked duck and dried fruit combination. If your taste buds don't agree with the black currant–flavored liqueur, consider moistening the duck and fruit with your favorite brand of bourbon. Or if you prefer not to add alcohol at all, use pure apple juice.

A nice Chianti, specifically an elegant Chianti Classico produced by Castello di Ama, would please the most precious palate. This wine with its supple fruit flavor and smooth finish is a perfect match for the abundance of flavors and textures provided by this salad.

Saffron Fettuccine with Broccoli, Grilled Sweet Onions, Smoked Tomatoes, and Lemon Vinaigrette

Serves 4

Smoked Tomatoes

3 large tomatoes (about 2¼ pounds), peeled,
   seeded, and cut in half

Saffron Fettuccine

big pinch of saffron (1.3 grams)
 2 tablespoons hot water
 2 cups all-purpose flour

 2 large eggs
½ tablespoon extra-virgin olive oil
½ teaspoon salt

Lemon Vinaigrette

zest and juice from 1 medium lemon
4 tablespoons cider vinegar
1 tablespoon Dijon-style mustard

1 cup extra-virgin olive oil
salt and freshly ground black pepper to taste

Salad Vegetables

1 large bunch broccoli (about 1½ pounds),
   stems trimmed
1 large sweet onion (about ¾ pound),
   peeled and cut into ½-inch-thick slices

 2 tablespoons extra-virgin olive oil
salt and freshly ground black pepper to taste
¼ pound watercress, trimmed, washed, and
   dried

❧

SMOKE THE TOMATOES

Line the top shelf of a smoker with parchment paper. Place the tomato halves, cut side down, on the shelf in the smoker and smoke for 1 to 1½ hours (depending on the desired intensity of flavor), turning them over halfway through the smoking time. Remove the tomatoes from the smoker and cut into ¼-inch cubes. Wrap in plastic wrap and refrigerate until needed.

If you don't have a smoker, you may grill the peeled and seeded tomato halves over a low wood or charcoal fire for a minute or two on each side. This will impart a light smoky flavor (albeit not as intense as that from the smoker).

MAKE THE SAFFRON FETTUCCINE DOUGH

In a cup-size container, steep the saffron in the hot water for 30 minutes.

Place 1¾ cups of flour on a clean, dry work surface or in a 7-quart bowl. Make a well in the center of the flour large enough to hold the eggs, saffron infusion, olive oil, and salt. Using a fork, combine the eggs, saffron, oil, and salt. When thoroughly mixed, use a fork to work the flour into the egg mixture, a small amount at a time. When enough flour has been added so that you can handle the dough, begin kneading by hand. Knead until all the flour has been incorporated, about 10 minutes. Wrap the dough in plastic wrap and set aside at room temperature for 1 hour.

MAKE THE LEMON VINAIGRETTE

While the dough is relaxing, make the vinaigrette. In a 3-quart stainless steel bowl, whisk together the lemon juice and zest, cider vinegar, and mustard. Slowly whisk in the olive oil in a slow, steady stream until incorporated. Season with salt and pepper. Cover with plastic wrap and set aside at room temperature until needed.

Equipment

paring knife
5-quart saucepan
colander
cook's knife
measuring spoons
measuring cup
vegetable peeler
smoker
parchment paper
plastic wrap
3-quart stainless steel bowl
whisk
pasta machine
colander
7-quart stainless steel bowl
3-quart saucepan
basting brush
charcoal grill
spatula
baking sheet

Grilled shrimp variation requires:
four 8-inch bamboo or metal skewers
tongs

Poached chicken variation requires:
large nonstick sauté pan

CUT AND COOK THE PASTA

Cut the pasta dough into 4 equal pieces. Roll and knead each piece through the pasta machine, using the extra ¼ cup of flour as necessary to prevent the dough from becoming sticky. Cut each sheet of dough into fettuccine.

Bring 3 quarts of salted water to a boil in a 5-quart saucepan over high heat. When boiling, add the fettuccine and cook, stirring frequently, until tender but slightly firm to the bite, about 1 to 1½ minutes. Drain the cooked fettuccine in a colander, then shake the colander to remove as much excess water from the fettuccine as possible. Transfer the well-drained fettuccine to a 7-quart stainless steel bowl. Vigorously whisk the vinaigrette and add ¾ cup to the pasta along with the smoked tomatoes. (Cover the remaining ¾ cup of vinaigrette and set aside until needed.) Season with salt and pepper, and toss to coat the fettuccine with the vinaigrette. Cover loosely with plastic wrap and set aside for up to 1 hour before serving.

PREPARE THE SALAD VEGETABLES

Trim the broccoli into florets. Bring 2 quarts of lightly salted water to a boil in a 3-quart saucepan over medium-high heat. Cook the broccoli in the boiling salted water until tender but still crunchy, about 2½ to 3 minutes. Transfer to a colander and drain thoroughly, then submerge in ice water to stop the cooking. Drain the broccoli again. Set aside until needed.

Brush the onion slices with the olive oil and season generously with salt and pepper. Grill the onion slices over a medium wood or charcoal fire until nicely charred and cooked through, about 3½ to 4 minutes on each side. Transfer the onions to a warm platter while arranging the salads.

ASSEMBLE THE SALAD

Divide and arrange the watercress, stem ends toward the center, in a ring, with the leaf ends near the outside edge of four 10- to 12-inch room-temperature soup or pasta plates. Place equal amounts of dressed fettuccine and smoked tomatoes inside the ring of watercress. Arrange an equal amount of broccoli florets in the center of each portion of fettuccine. Separate the onion slices into rings and place an equal amount around the broccoli on each salad. Vigorously whisk the remaining dressing and dress each salad with 2 to 3 tablespoons of vinaigrette. Serve immediately.

*G*rilled Skewer of Curry-Scented Shrimp Variation

1 pound large shrimp, peeled, deveined, and
  split in half lengthwise
1 tablespoon extra-virgin olive oil

salt and freshly ground black pepper to taste
$\frac{1}{2}$ teaspoon curry powder

Divide the shrimp into four 4-ounce portions. Skewer the shrimp on 4 skewers. Cover with plastic wrap and refrigerate until ready to grill.

Brush the skewers of shrimp with the olive oil. Season with salt and pepper, then evenly sprinkle the curry powder on the skewers. Grill the shrimp skewers over a medium wood or charcoal fire for $1\frac{1}{2}$ to 2 minutes on each side (a total of 3 to 4 minutes); be careful not to overcook because the shrimp can go from tender to tough in a matter of seconds. (The shrimp skewers may also be broiled in the oven. Cook for about the same amount of time.) Remove the shrimp from the skewers and position each portion around the broccoli on each salad. Serve immediately.

*C*hardonnay-Poached Chicken Breast Variation

4 4-ounce boneless, skinless chicken breasts
1 tablespoon fresh lemon juice
salt and freshly ground black pepper to taste
1 cup California or French chardonnay

$\frac{1}{2}$ cup water
1 medium lemon, very thinly sliced and
  seeds removed
a few sprigs fresh thyme

Trim any excess fat from the breasts. Sprinkle with the lemon juice and season with salt and pepper. Cover each breast with plastic wrap and refrigerate until needed.

Heat the chardonnay, water, sliced lemon, and thyme sprigs in a large nonstick sauté pan over medium-high heat. When the liquid begins to simmer, add the chicken breasts, then cover with a piece of parchment paper cut to fit the inside dimension of the pan. Poach the chicken for 15 minutes, adjusting the heat as necessary to keep the liquid at a simmer. Use a pair of tongs to turn the chicken over in the poaching liquid about halfway through the cooking time. Remove the pan from the heat. Discard the parchment paper, lemon slices, thyme, and poaching liquid. Transfer the chicken breasts to a cutting board and cut them into ½-inch slices on a long bias. Fan the breasts around the broccoli on each salad. Serve immediately.

The Chef's Touch

SMOKED TOMATOES were dubbed "smokers" by one of The Trellis cooks years ago. I had recently obtained a smoker for our kitchen but failed to acquire the expertise to operate this relatively fancy piece of equipment. As you might suspect, my first attempt at smoking (and it was tomatoes) ended with as much smoke in the kitchen as in the smoker, but the tomatoes picked up intense flavor and a nickname.

The smoked tomatoes may be refrigerated for several days. Cool the chopped "smokers" for 30 minutes at room temperature, then store in a tightly sealed plastic container for up to a week before using.

Saffron, indispensable to the flavor and appearance of international dishes such as bouillabaisse and paella, is also an essential element in this salad. The vibrant color and flavor of the saffron fettuccine harmonizes with the smoky flavor of the tomatoes and the acidity of the vinaigrette. It will cost you a few bucks—we paid $11.98 at the supermarket for 1.3 grams of saffron—but it is well worth the price.

For advance preparation of the fettuccine, toss the cut fettuccine with ½ cup of cornmeal (to prevent the strands from sticking to each other during refrigeration), then place the pasta on a baking sheet lined with parchment paper. Cover tightly with plastic wrap and refrigerate until ready to cook, up to 3 days. Be sure to shake the cornmeal off the fettuccine before cooking it in boiling water.

The Lemon Vinaigrette recipe yields 1½ cups. The vinaigrette may be kept at room temperature for several hours before using or refrigerated in a covered, noncorrosive container for 2 to 3 days. If refrigerated, allow the vinaigrette to return to room temperature and whisk vigorously before using.

One large bunch of watercress, about ½ pound as purchased, should yield ¼ pound, trimmed (cut away about ½ inch of the stem ends), washed, and dried leaves. For crisp greens, spin-dry the washed watercress in a salad spinner.

Watercress withers in a short period of time (what we get at The Trellis comes packed in ice). Purchase only what you need and can use within a day or two.

Fresh shrimp are very perishable, so it is best to keep them covered with crushed ice in the refrigerator for no more than 1 or 2 days of purchase. If using frozen shrimp, thaw under cold running water and use on the same day.

It may seem easy to be intimidated in making the right wine selection here because of all the flavors going on. I accept the challenge and suggest a big buttery and oaky California chardonnay.

Spicy Rice Spring Rolls with Asian Vegetable Slaw and Toasted Pumpkin Seed Dressing

Serves 4

Toasted Pumpkin Seed Dressing

1 cup Chinese pumpkin seeds
4 tablespoons rice wine vinegar
2 tablespoons fresh lemon juice
2 tablespoons creamy peanut butter
¼ teaspoon hot sauce
¾ cup peanut oil
salt to taste

Asian Vegetable Slaw

½ pound long beans, trimmed and cut into
   3-inch-long sections
½ medium head Chinese cabbage (about
   1 pound), discolored outer leaves
   removed, cored, and sliced widthwise
   ⅛ inch thick
½ pound daikon, peeled and cut lengthwise
   into sticks 3 inches long and ⅛ inch thick
1 medium red onion (about 6 ounces),
   peeled and thinly sliced
Toasted Pumpkin Seed Dressing
salt and freshly ground black pepper to taste

Spicy Rice Spring Rolls

1 cup plus 1 tablespoon peanut oil
1 teaspoon minced garlic
1 teaspoon minced ginger
1 tablespoon minced shallots
¾ cup converted rice
salt and freshly ground black pepper to taste
1½ cups hot Vegetable Stock (see page 26)
1 teaspoon minced fresh cilantro
1 teaspoon hot sauce
1 teaspoon minced lemon zest
1 teaspoon sesame oil
1 teaspoon soy sauce
1 cup chopped scallions (about 1 bunch
   with root ends trimmed)
¾ cup fresh Crunchy Sprouts
   (see page 160)
2 tablespoons granulated sugar
8 circles rice paper

Salad Greens

½ pound radicchio, cored, trimmed, cut into
  1-inch pieces, washed, and dried
½ pound curly endive, cored, trimmed, cut
  into ¾-inch pieces, washed, and dried

ॐ

MAKE THE TOASTED
PUMPKIN SEED DRESSING
Preheat the oven to 325 degrees Fahrenheit.

Toast the pumpkin seeds on a baking sheet in the preheated oven for 15 minutes. Remove from the oven and cool to room temperature. Place ½ cup of cooled pumpkin seeds in the bowl of a food processor fitted with a metal blade; save the other ½ cup to garnish the salad. Process the seeds for 30 seconds, until powdered.

In a 3-quart stainless steel bowl, whisk together the rice wine vinegar, lemon juice, peanut butter, and hot sauce until smooth. Add the peanut oil in a slow, steady stream while whisking until incorporated. Add powdered pumpkin seeds and salt as needed and whisk to combine. Cover with plastic wrap and set aside at room temperature until needed.

PREPARE THE ASIAN
VEGETABLE SLAW
Heat 3 quarts of salted water in a 5-quart saucepan over medium-high heat. When the water boils, add the long beans. Cook the beans until tender but slightly crisp, about 4 to 6 minutes depending on the thickness of the bean. Drain the beans in a colander, then immediately plunge them into ice water to stop the cooking and keep the beans bright green. Remove from the ice water and drain thoroughly. Transfer the beans to a 7-quart stainless steel bowl.

Add the Chinese cabbage, daikon, red onion, and ¾ cup toasted pumpkin seed dressing. (Cover the remaining ¾ cup of dressing and set aside at room temperature until needed.) Combine the vegetables with the dressing (I suggest you wear a

Equipment

measuring cup
measuring spoons
paring knife
cook's knife
cutting board
vegetable peeler
salad spinner
baking sheet
food processor with metal
  blade
3-quart stainless steel bowl
whisk
plastic wrap
5-quart saucepan
colander
7-quart stainless steel bowl
3-quart saucepan with lid
two 5-quart stainless steel
  bowls
1-quart stainless steel bowl
rubber spatula
paper towels
large nonstick sauté pan
tongs

*Shredded pork variation
  requires:*
slotted kitchen spoon

*Tuna burger variation
  requires:*
small nonstick sauté pan
meat grinder with coarse
  grinding plate
medium nonstick sauté
  pan
spatula

pair of plastic food handler's gloves). Add salt and pepper as needed and combine. Cover with plastic wrap and refrigerate until serving time (up to 24 hours).

P R E P A R E　 T H E　 S P I C Y　 R I C E　 S P R I N G　 R O L L S

Heat 1 tablespoon of peanut oil in a 3-quart saucepan over medium-high heat. When the oil is hot, add the garlic, ginger, and shallots. Sauté for 30 seconds. Add the rice and stir to incorporate. Season with salt and pepper. Add the hot vegetable stock and stir to combine. Bring to a simmer, then lower the heat to medium, cover the pan, and cook the rice for 20 minutes. Remove from the heat and transfer the rice to a 5-quart stainless steel bowl.

In a 1-quart stainless steel bowl, whisk together the cilantro, hot sauce, lemon zest, sesame oil, and soy sauce. Pour over the rice, and add the scallions and Crunchy Sprouts. Use a rubber spatula to combine the ingredients thoroughly. Cool, uncovered, in the refrigerator while preparing the rice paper.

In a 5-quart stainless steel bowl, dissolve the sugar in 2 quarts of warm water. Soak 1 circle of rice paper in the warm water for 1 minute. Remove the rice paper from the water and hold it between individual sheets of wet paper towels. Repeat with the remaining circles of rice paper, working with 1 at a time, until all 8 have been soaked and placed in between wet paper towels.

Place 1 circle of rice paper on a clean, dry work surface; keep the other circles moistened between the layers of wet paper towels. Place ½ cup of the spicy rice mixture on half of the rice paper, keeping the mixture about ½ inch away from the edge of the paper. Fold the bottom half of the rice paper over the spicy rice mixture, then fold in the sides toward the center. Roll the spring roll toward the open end to seal. Repeat this procedure until all 8 spring rolls have been assembled.

Preheat the oven to 225 degrees Fahrenheit.

Heat the remaining 1 cup of peanut oil in a large nonstick sauté pan over medium-high heat. When the oil is hot, place 4 spring rolls, seam side down, in the hot oil and fry for 4 to 5 minutes. Use tongs to turn the rolls as necessary until the rolls are uniformly golden brown. Transfer the fried rolls to a baking sheet lined with paper towels and place in the preheated oven. Fry the remaining 4 rolls in the hot oil, then transfer to the baking sheet with the other rolls and keep in the oven while assembling the salads.

A S S E M B L E　 T H E　 S A L A D

Combine the radicchio and curly endive. Divide and arrange the greens on four 10- to 12-inch room-temperature plates. Dress the greens with 2 to 3 tablespoons of toasted pumpkin seed dressing. Place an equal amount of Asian vegetable slaw on each plate of greens. Place 2 spring rolls around the outside edge of the slaw. Sprinkle the remaining pumpkin seeds over each salad. Serve immediately.

Stir-Fried Shredded Pork with Peanuts Variation

½ cup unsalted peanuts
1 tablespoon creamy peanut butter
1 tablespoon rice wine vinegar
1 tablespoon soy sauce
1 tablespoon granulated sugar

1 pound boneless pork loin, trimmed of fat
   and membrane, and cut into very thin
   slices about 3 inches long and ½ inch wide
salt and freshly ground black pepper to taste
1 tablespoon peanut oil

Preheat the oven to 325 degrees Fahrenheit.

Toast the peanuts on a baking sheet in the preheated oven for 10 minutes. Remove the nuts from the oven and set aside to cool at room temperature. When the nuts are cool, chop them into ¼-inch pieces. Set aside.

In a 5-quart stainless steel bowl, whisk together the peanut butter, rice wine vinegar, soy sauce, and sugar until smooth. Season the pork strips with salt and pepper. Place the pork strips in the bowl with the peanut mixture and use a rubber spatula to combine until the pork is coated with the mixture.

Heat the peanut oil in a large nonstick sauté pan over high heat. When the oil is hot, add the pork pieces and stir-fry about 2½ minutes to 3 minutes, until browned and cooked through (but not dried out). Add the chopped peanuts and stir to combine. Remove from the heat. Use a slotted spoon to place an equal amount of pork and peanuts on each salad. Serve immediately.

ᛋ

Pan-Seared Lemon Tuna Burger Variation

1 tablespoon peanut oil
¾ cup finely diced red onion
salt and freshly ground black pepper to taste
1 tablespoon fresh lemon juice

1 tablespoon minced lemon zest
1 pound fresh tuna fillet, cut into 1-inch
  cubes

Heat the peanut oil in a medium nonstick sauté pan over medium heat. When the oil is hot, add the red onion, season with salt and pepper, and cook for 3 minutes, until tender. Remove from the heat, add the lemon juice and zest, and stir to combine. Transfer the onion mixture to a large dish and cool, uncovered, in the refrigerator for 15 minutes.

Grind the tuna pieces through a meat grinder fitted with a coarse grinding plate into a 5-quart stainless steel bowl. Add the cooled onion mixture and gently but thoroughly combine. Gently form the tuna mixture into four 4-ounce burgers, 1 inch thick. Cook immediately or cover with plastic wrap and refrigerate until needed (up to 24 hours).

Heat a medium nonstick sauté pan over medium-high heat. When the pan is hot, sear the tuna burgers for 2½ to 3 minutes on each side for medium-rare or longer on each side for well done. Place a burger on each salad. Serve immediately.

The Chef's Touch

PUMPKIN SEEDS remind me of my days as a paperboy in the late 50s when I had a route that wove a maze through the tenement houses on our end of Woonsocket, Rhode Island. My route was easier to walk than bike because of the number of stops in a relatively small area, plus an endless number of steps to climb in each tenement. After all that walking and climbing, I was in need of an energy boost and would head to Dube's Spa, the neighborhood variety store. On those rare occasions when I didn't eat a chocolate bar, I would down a Coke and a box of salted pumpkin seeds. Not the pearly green pumpkin seeds I

The Chef's Touch

recommend for this salad, but the moldy gray, salt-crusted, gum-ripping un-shelled seeds found in the likes of Dube's Spa then and 7-Elevens now across the country.

Don't get your seeds for this salad from 7-Eleven. Instead, you can find Chinese pumpkin seeds in specialty stores and the bulk foods section at the market. Look for seeds with the hulls removed that are smooth, pale green, and not salted. They are well worth the extra expense. Incidentally, I recently paid about thirty cents per ounce at the market for seeds without the hull while the salted seeds in the hull are retailing for fifty cents an ounce at 7-Eleven. Figure that one out!

The Toasted Pumpkin Seed Dressing recipe yields about 1½ cups of dressing. The dressing may be kept at room temperature for a couple of hours before using or refrigerated in a covered, noncorrosive container for 2 to 3 days. If refrigerated, return the dressing to room temperature before using; the dressing remains emulsified, so there is no need to whisk.

Long beans, also known as yard-long beans, are available year-round at most Asian markets. Select younger beans that are 12 to 18 inches long (they do grow up to 3 feet, hence the alternate name) or choose snap beans as a substitute. No matter which bean you use, be certain not to overcook. Their flavor is optimal when they are tender but slightly crisp.

The type of Chinese cabbage used for this recipe is also known as Napa cabbage and celery cabbage, and should not be confused with another type of Chinese cabbage called bok choy. Chinese cabbage has an elongated head of tightly packed leaves and is delicious uncooked. Once dressed with the Toasted Pumpkin Seed Dressing, it will lose a significant amount of volume, so don't be overwhelmed by the quantity when it is first sliced.

The Asian radish, known as daikon, has a wonderful sweet and very subtle peppery taste. I like its flavor as well as its crunchy texture. Creamy white and crisp, it keeps its shape and contrasts in color with the beans, cabbage, and onions.

For the lemon zest, use a sharp vegetable peeler to remove the skin from a lemon (only the colored part of the skin should be removed, not the bitter

(continued on next page)

white pith under the skin). Once removed, the skin may be minced with a sharp knife, finely chopped, or sliced. Other methods work, such as using a box grater, but they do not produce zest that is as nicely defined.

Fresh Crunchy Sprouts are a delicious mélange of sprouted fresh green peas, cow peas, red lentils, garbanzo beans, and mung beans. You will find them packed in a 4-ounce plastic container (1½ cups by volume) in the fresh produce section at the supermarket.

These spring rolls are worth the hard work, but if time is a consideration, the rolls are delicious unfried—or serve the rice mixture without the rice paper all together. In this case, the cooked rice mixture may be kept at room temperature for up to 3 hours before serving. Or cool to room temperature and then refrigerate in a covered, noncorrosive container for a couple of days.

Although exotic in appearance, rice paper is simply a cooked flat noodle. As purchased, the paper is stiff and brittle, and must be soaked to make it flexible and foldable. The assembled spring rolls may be kept at room temperature for a couple of hours before cooking if covered with wet sheets of paper towels.

One medium head of radicchio, about ½ pound as purchased, should yield 6 ounces of prepared leaves. One small head of curly endive, about ½ pound as purchased, should yield ¼ pound of prepared greens. For crisp greens, separately spin-dry the washed radicchio and curly endive in a salad spinner.

I would have enjoyed a Chinese beer with this salad, but the fridge at Ganache Hill contained Pete's Wicked Ale the day we tested this recipe. I almost always select wine to accompany food, but sometimes the recipe and the mood call for a chilled frothy brew. I thought the Pete's slightly hoppy flavor and clean finish provided a foil to the myriad of spicy flavors in the salad.

Warm Grits Cake with Black-eyed Pea, Tomato, and Corn Relish, Curly Endive, Red Leaf Lettuce, and Peanut Oil Dressing

Serves 4

Grits Cake

2 teaspoons peanut oil
2 cups Vegetable Stock (page 26)
1 cup heavy cream
2 tablespoons unsalted butter
1 teaspoon salt

½ teaspoon freshly ground black pepper
1 cup stone-ground white grits
¼ cup grated cheddar cheese
½ cup fresh white corn

Peanut Oil Dressing

1 cup unsalted peanuts
6 tablespoons cider vinegar
1 tablespoon fresh lemon juice

¾ cup peanut oil
salt and freshly ground black pepper to taste
2 tablespoons chopped fresh parsley

Black-eyed Pea, Tomato, and Corn Relish

1½ cups dried black-eyed peas, washed, picked over, and soaked for 12 hours in 2 quarts cold water
1 tablespoon salt
Peanut Oil Dressing
3 medium tomatoes (about 1¼ pounds), peeled, seeded, and chopped into ¼-inch pieces

1¼ cups fresh white corn
1 bunch scallions, cleaned, trimmed, and thinly sliced
salt and freshly ground black pepper to taste

Equipment
measuring spoons
measuring cup
box grater
cook's knife
cutting board
colander
3-quart plastic container
paring knife
salad spinner
9½- by 1½-inch round cake pan
pastry brush
parchment paper
3-quart saucepan
2 wire whisks (1 stiff)
rubber spatula
cooling rack
nonstick baking sheet
food processor with metal blade
3-quart stainless steel bowl
plastic wrap
5-quart saucepan
7-quart stainless steel bowl
serrated slicer

Catfish variation requires:
pie tin
large nonstick sauté pan
tongs
paper towels

Rabbit variation requires:
boning knife
large nonstick sauté pan
slotted kitchen spoon

Salad Greens

¾ pound red leaf lettuce, cored, separated
 into leaves, washed, and dried
½ pound curly endive, cored, trimmed, cut
 into ½-inch pieces, washed, and dried

PREPARE THE GRITS CAKE

Brush the bottom and sides of a 9½- by 1½-inch round cake pan with 1 teaspoon of peanut oil. Line the pan with an 8-inch square sheet of parchment paper. Brush the parchment paper with the remaining teaspoon of peanut oil. Set aside.

Heat the vegetable stock, heavy cream, butter, salt, and pepper in a 3-quart saucepan over medium heat. Bring the mixture to a boil, then add the grits in a slow, steady stream while stirring constantly with a rigid wire whisk. Continue to stir while cooking the mixture for 6 minutes, until very thick. Remove the grits mixture from the heat and add the cheese, stirring until the cheese melts and is incorporated. Add the corn and stir to combine.

Pour the grits mixture into the prepared cake pan, and spread it evenly. Place the cake pan on a cooling rack and keep at room temperature to cool for 30 minutes, then place the pan in the refrigerator for 1 hour, until the cake is thoroughly chilled. While the grits cake is cooling and chilling, make the dressing and relish.

MAKE THE PEANUT OIL DRESSING

Preheat the oven to 325 degrees Fahrenheit.

Toast the peanuts on a nonstick baking sheet in the preheated oven for 10 to 12 minutes, until golden brown. Remove from the oven and cool to room temperature. Set aside ½ cup of peanuts to garnish the salad. Place the remaining ½ cup in the bowl of a food processor fitted with a metal blade. Process the peanuts until finely chopped, about 1 minute. Transfer the chopped peanuts to a 3-quart stainless steel bowl. Add the cider vinegar and lemon juice, and whisk until combined. Add the peanut oil in a slow, steady stream while whisking until incorporated. Season with salt and pepper. Add the chopped parsley and stir to combine. Cover the dressing tightly with plastic wrap and set aside at room temperature until needed.

P R E P A R E   T H E   B L A C K - E Y E D   P E A ,   T O M A T O , A N D   C O R N   R E L I S H

Drain the soaked black-eyed peas in a colander. Rinse the peas with cold water and drain thoroughly before cooking.

Bring 2 quarts of water and 1 tablespoon of salt to a boil in a 5-quart saucepan over high heat. Add the black-eyed peas. Adjust the heat and simmer the peas about 40 minutes, until tender but slightly firm to the bite. Drain the cooked peas in a colander, then transfer to a 7-quart stainless steel bowl. Vigorously whisk the peanut oil dressing, then add ¾ cup to the black-eyed peas. (Cover the remaining ¾ cup of dressing with plastic wrap and set aside at room temperature until needed.) Add the chopped tomatoes, white corn, and scallions to the black-eyed peas. Use a rubber spatula to stir the ingredients until combined. Adjust the seasoning. Cover the bowl with plastic wrap and set aside for up to 2 hours at room temperature. Or cool to room temperature and then refrigerate in a covered, noncorrosive container for up to 2 days before serving.

F I N I S H   A N D   A S S E M B L E   T H E   S A L A D

Preheat the oven to 350 degrees Fahrenheit.

Remove the grits cake from the refrigerator and from the cake pan. Use a serrated slicer to cut the cake into 16 equal slices. Place the slices in two rows, evenly spaced, on a nonstick baking sheet. Place the baking sheet on the center rack of the preheated oven and heat the cake slices for 10 to 12 minutes until hot throughout. Lower the oven temperature to 200 degrees Fahrenheit and keep the grits cake slices warm while assembling the salads.

Divide and arrange the red leaf lettuce on four 10- to 12-inch room-temperature plates. Divide and arrange the curly endive on top of the red leaf lettuce. Vigorously whisk the peanut oil dressing. Sprinkle the greens with 2 tablespoons of the dressing. Place equal amounts of the black-eyed pea, tomato, and corn relish on top of the greens. Sprinkle each portion of relish with 1 tablespoon of dressing. Sprinkle peanuts on each salad. Place 4 grits cake slices around each salad. Serve immediately.

❦

*P*anfried Catfish Variation

2 tablespoons fresh lemon juice

¾ pound skinless farm-raised catfish fillets,
   cut into strips 4 to 5 inches long and 1 to
   1½ inches wide

salt and freshly ground black pepper to taste

¾ cup whole milk

1 teaspoon hot sauce

½ cup all-purpose flour

½ cup white cornmeal

1 teaspoon salt

¼ teaspoon ground cayenne pepper

1½ cups peanut oil

Sprinkle the lemon juice over the catfish fillet strips. Lightly season with salt and black pepper. Cook immediately or cover with plastic wrap and refrigerate until needed (up to 24 hours).

In a 3-quart stainless steel bowl, whisk together the milk and hot sauce. Combine the all-purpose flour, cornmeal, 1 teaspoon of salt, and cayenne pepper in a pie tin or similar-size shallow dish.

Place the catfish strips one at a time in the milk and hot sauce combination, then in the flour and cornmeal mixture, and coat them lightly but evenly with the mixture. Transfer each catfish strip to a baking sheet or platter.

Heat the peanut oil in a large nonstick sauté pan over medium heat. When the oil is hot, place the catfish in the pan and fry for 8 minutes, turning as necessary, until lightly golden brown on all sides. Transfer the fillets to a baking sheet lined with paper towels. Allow the panfried catfish to stand for a minute or so, until any excess grease is absorbed by the paper. Arrange an equal amount of panfried catfish strips on each salad. Serve immediately or place the catfish in a preheated 200-degree Fahrenheit oven to keep warm for up to 30 minutes.

Sautéed Rabbit and Country Ham Variation

1 2½-pound dressed rabbit
salt and freshly ground black pepper to taste
1 tablespoon peanut oil

¼ pound country ham, cut into thin strips
1 bunch scallions, cleaned, trimmed, and
    chopped

Bone the rabbit (or ask the butcher to do this for you). Remove all the meat (except from the scrawny front legs, which have negligible meat). Trim away all tendons and silverskin membrane from the loins, tenderloins, hind leg, and thigh sections. Cut the trimmed meat into ¾-inch pieces. The rabbit may be cooked immediately or covered with plastic wrap and refrigerated for up to 24 hours.

Lightly season the rabbit with salt and pepper. Heat the peanut oil in a large nonstick sauté pan over medium-high heat. When the oil is hot, add the rabbit and cook, turning frequently, about 3 minutes, until lightly browned on all sides. Add the country ham strips and scallions, and heat for 1 more minute. Remove the pan from the heat and place an equal amount of rabbit and ham onto each salad. Serve immediately.

The Chef's Touch

MY FIRST TASTE of grits was disgusting, and I had to stand in line to get them! But those gelatinous instant grits served on a metal tray at the Marine training base in Parris Island were a far cry from the stone-ground grits I enjoy today, more than three decades later. Back then, after too many mounds of Marine Corps grits, I vowed never to touch them again. But after moving to Williamsburg, Virginia, in 1970, one day my taste buds were embraced by a grits soufflé so luxuriant, warm, and deliciously textural that I was transformed. The Marine Corps grits had taken on the sensual pleasure of R & R in Bangkok! The world needs to know that the lush corn flavor and complex

(continued on next page)

texture of stone-ground grits are light-years away from the monochromatic mush of instant grits. If everyone who served grits converted to stone-ground, more people would move south or join the Marine Corps.

Since opening The Trellis in 1980, grits have made several appearances on our seasonal dinner menus. One of my favorite recipes is barbecued shrimp with corn relish served on diminutive *crispy* grits cakes. The grits cake for our salad is light and creamy instead of crispy, and more dense than the soufflé that converted me. And it is delicious! In case you're not familiar with grits, they are milled from white corn and, at their most basic, are cooked like oatmeal. But as you can see from this recipe, good-quality stone-ground grits are quite versatile.

The Peanut Oil Dressing recipe yields 1½ cups. The dressing may be kept at room temperature for several hours before using or refrigerated in a covered, noncorrosive container for up to 2 days. If refrigerated, return the dressing to room temperature and whisk vigorously before using.

I don't remember if I ever ate black-eyed peas in the Marine Corps (I'm sure they would have come from a can and have been cooked to an unrecognizable mush, too—sorry, Chesty). Perhaps I first tasted them as a student at The Culinary Institute of America, but I do know that I love them when fresh or dried, not canned *à la* the Marine Corps. Dried black-eyed peas are very easily cooked and are always available. Fresh black-eyed peas (in some areas of the South they are still called cowpeas) need to be shucked and are available primarily during the summer season, but I see them at the market at the end of the year. (They are eaten in the South on New Year's Day to bring good luck.)

One medium head of red leaf lettuce, about ¾ pound as purchased, should yield ½ pound of prepared leaves. And one small head of curly endive, about ½ pound as purchased, should yield ¼ pound of prepared greens. For crisp greens, separately spin-dry the washed red leaf lettuce leaves and the curly endive pieces in a lettuce spinner.

You should be able to find fresh rabbit at the market. The most tender meat comes from young rabbits weighing 2½ pounds or less. Although you can use frozen rabbit for this recipe, the delicate and delicious flavor of the meat is somewhat lost in the deep freeze.

The Chef's Touch

We have purchased the country ham we serve at The Trellis from the same source since opening in 1980. The Edwards family (see Sources, page 225) has been in business producing this unique product for many more years than that, and the secret to their success is that they make country ham the old-fashioned way . . . slowly. The hams are salt-cured on racks in a large refrigerated room, versus being injected with a cure or dipped in a vat of salt brine, as is done with some other brands. Additionally, they smoke the hams (real smoke, not an injection) and then age them for several months.

A very pleasant and logical wine to enjoy with this salad (especially if you appreciate its southern influence) would be the Williamsburg Winery Act 12 Chardonnay. Several of the vintages of this wine have garnered honors as well as national attention. This carefully crafted wine offers opulent fruit the way southerners offer hospitality. Come on down and try it for yourself.

Beets, Carrots, and Radishes Cut Japanese Style with Buckwheat Noodles, Screaming Peanuts, and Soy-Ginger Dressing

Serves 4

Buckwheat Noodles

1 cup all-purpose flour
¼ cup buckwheat flour
2 large eggs

2 tablespoons peanut oil
½ teaspoon salt
salt and freshly ground black pepper to taste

Soy-Ginger Dressing

4 tablespoons rice wine vinegar
1 tablespoon soy sauce
1 tablespoon finely minced ginger
1 tablespoon granulated sugar

1 teaspoon peanut oil
½ teaspoon ground white pepper
dash hot sauce
1 cup mayonnaise

Screaming Peanuts

1 tablespoon peanut oil
1 tablespoon soy sauce
1 teaspoon granulated sugar
3 to 4 teaspoons hot sauce

dash or two chili oil
1 cup unsalted peanut halves
salt to taste

Salad Greens and Garnish

1 small daikon radish (about ½ pound), peeled
½ pound carrots, peeled
2 to 3 small beets (about ½ pound), peeled

½ pound radicchio, cored, trimmed, washed, and dried
1 bunch chives, cut into 2-inch-long pieces

୬

PREPARE THE BUCKWHEAT NOODLE DOUGH

Combine ¾ cup of all-purpose flour and the buckwheat flour on a clean, dry work surface or in a 7-quart bowl. Make a well in the center of the flour large enough to hold the eggs, 1 tablespoon of peanut oil (the remaining 1 tablespoon will be used to coat the pasta after it is cooked), and ½ teaspoon of salt. Using a fork, combine the eggs, oil, and salt. When thoroughly mixed, use the fork to begin working the flour into the egg mixture, a small amount at a time. Once the dough is stiff enough to handle, knead it by hand until all the flour has been incorporated, about 10 minutes. Wrap the dough in plastic wrap and set aside at room temperature for 1 hour while you make the dressing and toast the peanuts.

MAKE THE SOY-GINGER DRESSING

In a 3-quart stainless steel bowl, vigorously whisk together the rice wine vinegar, soy sauce, ginger, sugar, 1 teaspoon peanut oil, pepper, and hot sauce. Add the mayonnaise and whisk until smooth. Cover tightly with plastic wrap and refrigerate until needed.

MAKE THE SCREAMING PEANUTS

Preheat the oven to 325 degrees Fahrenheit.

Heat the peanut oil in a medium nonstick sauté pan over medium heat. When the oil is hot, remove the pan from the heat, add the soy sauce, sugar, hot sauce (you decide how loud!), and chili oil. Whisk to combine. Add the peanuts and toss to coat. Spread the peanuts out on a nonstick baking sheet. Place the baking sheet in the preheated oven and toast the peanuts for 12 minutes. Remove from the oven, then transfer the peanuts to a baking sheet lined with paper towels. Season to taste with salt while the peanuts are still warm. Cool the peanuts to room temperature, then store in a tightly sealed plastic container at room temperature until ready to use.

Equipment

measuring cup
measuring spoons
paring knife
cook's knife
cutting board
vegetable peeler
salad spinner
plastic wrap
3-quart stainless steel bowl
whisk
medium nonstick sauté pan
2 baking sheets (1 nonstick)
pasta machine
5-quart saucepan
tongs
colander
Japanese turning slicer
three 2-quart plastic containers

Scallop variation requires:
large nonstick sauté pan
5-quart stainless steel bowl
slotted kitchen spoon

Pork variation requires:
basting brush
large nonstick sauté pan
serrated slicer

CUT AND COOK THE PASTA

Cut the pasta dough into 4 equal pieces. Roll and knead each portion of dough through the pasta machine, using the remaining ¼ cup of flour as necessary to prevent the dough from becoming sticky. Cut each sheet of dough into angel hair.

Bring 3 quarts of salted water to a boil in a 5-quart saucepan over high heat. Add the pasta and cook, stirring frequently, about 1½ minutes, until tender but slightly firm to the bite. Drain the pasta in a colander, then cool under running cold water. Drain thoroughly. Transfer the pasta to a 7-quart stainless steel bowl and add the remaining 1 tablespoon of peanut oil. Season with salt and pepper, then toss to coat the pasta. Cover with plastic wrap and set aside at room temperature for up to 2 hours before serving.

FINISH AND ASSEMBLE THE SALAD

Trim the ends of the daikon, carrots, and beets so that the ends are flat. Cut the vegetables (the daikon first, followed by the carrots, and finishing with the beets) into long, thin strands using a Japanese turning slicer. Place each cut vegetable in a separate plastic container. Assemble the salads immediately or cover the containers and refrigerate until needed (up to several hours).

Divide and arrange the beet strands in a ring near the outside edge of each of 4 room-temperature 10- to 12-inch plates. Divide and arrange the carrot strands inside the ring of beets, pushing the carrot strands toward the edge of the beets. Follow the same procedure with the daikon. Form a cup of radicchio leaves in the center of each salad. Fill each radicchio cup with an equal amount of buckwheat pasta. Dress each salad with 4 to 5 tablespoons of soy-ginger dressing. Sprinkle the screaming peanuts and chives over each salad. Serve immediately.

Stir-Fried Sea Scallops with Horseradish and Chives Variation

1½ pounds sea scallops, side muscle removed
salt and freshly ground black pepper to taste
2 tablespoons peanut oil

2 tablespoons grated fresh horseradish
2 tablespoons rice wine
1 bunch fresh chives, cut into 3-inch pieces

Place the scallops in a 3-quart stainless steel bowl and season with salt and pepper. Sprinkle the peanut oil over the scallops and toss to coat.

Heat a large nonstick sauté pan or wok over high heat. When the pan is hot, add the scallops and sear, turning only once, until golden, about 2 to 2½ minutes. Add the horseradish and rice wine, and stir to mix. Stir-fry for 1 more minute. Remove the pan from the heat and immediately transfer the scallops to a 5-quart stainless steel bowl. Add the chives and toss to combine. Using a slotted kitchen spoon, place an equal amount of scallops on each salad. Serve immediately.

※

*B*lackstrap-and-Honey-Roasted Pork *Tenderloin Variation*

1 tablespoon blackstrap molasses
½ tablespoon honey
1 14-ounce pork tenderloin, trimmed

salt and freshly ground black pepper to taste
1 tablespoon dry mustard

Preheat the oven to 350 degrees Fahrenheit.

In a small bowl, whisk the molasses and honey until combined.

Liberally season the pork tenderloin with salt and pepper. Sprinkle the dry mustard over the pork, coating all sides.

Heat a large nonstick sauté pan over medium-high heat. When the pan is hot, add the pork tenderloin and brown on all sides, turning as necessary, about 5 minutes. Transfer the tenderloin to a nonstick baking sheet with sides. Baste the tenderloin on all sides with the molasses mixture. Place in the preheated oven and roast for 10 minutes, basting again about halfway through the roasting time. Remove the pork from the oven and baste one more time. Transfer the pork to a cutting board and use a sharp slicer to cut the meat on the bias into 16 to 20 slices ¼ inch thick. Place 4 to 5 slices on each salad. Serve immediately.

The Chef's Touch

AT THE Trellis in the early 80s, we made all types of flavored pastas, from traditional to extraordinary. Tarragon, beet, and even pumpkin found their way into our pasta noodles. In fact, we would joke that if it didn't move, we would make pasta out of it!

I clearly remember tasting my first fresh buckwheat noodle during the early pasta experimentation. I was not aware of my allergy to the buckwheat until I swallowed one solitary noodle. After an alarming choking sensation in my throat, I pushed the plate away and have avoided it ever since (even though two instances of inadvertent buckwheat ingestion have reminded me that the allergy remains). I feel fortunate that this is my only food allergy (apart from the sensitivity to the penicillin in blue cheeses), and from researching the subject I now know that few people are sensitive to buckwheat. On the other side of the coin, a significant number of people have gluten allergies, so they can quite often enjoy products made from buckwheat (which is an herb rather than a cereal grain). For the handful of people who are sensitive to buckwheat, I suggest substituting whole wheat flour to make the noodles for this recipe.

You can find buckwheat flour at most health food stores and well-stocked supermarkets. For advance preparation of the buckwheat noodles, toss the cut noodles with ½ cup of cornmeal (to prevent the strands from sticking to each other during refrigeration), then place the noodles on a baking sheet lined with parchment paper. Cover tightly with plastic wrap and refrigerate for up to 3 days, until ready to cook. Be sure to shake the cornmeal off the noodles before cooking them in boiling water.

The Soy-Ginger Dressing recipe yields 1½ cups. The dressing may be stored in a covered, noncorrosive container in the refrigerator for 2 to 3 days.

I admit to a bit of hyperbole regarding the name of the peanuts. They have a bit of a kick, but unless you are a real "heat" wimp, you will probably find them more subtle than searing. You may, of course, up the ante with 1 to 2 teaspoons more of the hot sauce, as well as an additional dash or two of the chili oil (now can you hear the screaming?).

Daikon, also known as Oriental radish, is available year-round. The size, texture, and flavor can vary immensely. Select the elongated (carrot-shaped) white variety, which has the firm texture needed for cutting on the turning slicer and additionally has a pleasant sweet and peppery flavor.

One medium head of radicchio, about ½ pound as purchased, should yield 6 ounces of prepared leaves. For crisp radicchio, spin-dry the washed leaves in a salad spinner. We have found radicchio to be available year-round.

High-quality sea scallops are unfortunately becoming more and more difficult to locate. During the last few years I have been dismayed at the proliferation of "dipped" scallops, a sodium-based treatment that preserves the shelf life of the scallop but inhibits the flavor and makes them rubbery. Scallops that have been dipped have a soapy appearance and do not adhere to each other as fresh scallops do.

If handling the gnarly and earthy horseradish root puts you off, you may substitute a bit of preserved bottled horseradish or wasabi, the pungent green-colored Japanese horseradish.

With the pork option for this salad, be sure to select a high-grade blackstrap molasses. We use Plantation "The Original" Brand at The Trellis. This brand has a refined taste not found in other molasseses we have tried.

I am challenged in making a wine selection for this salad. At first glance the distinctly different flavors coming from so many of the ingredients seem to exclude many wines. However, the various nuances of most properly vinified wines give us a limitless number of potential pairings. Choose a white or red wine with a bit of spice, a good balance of acidity, and a smooth but not overwhelming amount of fruit. I would select from the current Trellis wine list the Sancerre Clos La Perriere or the Domaine Drouhin Oregon Pinot Noir. Enjoy.

Sliced Beets with Curly Endive, Red Bliss Potato Salad, Honey Mustard Roasted Walnuts, and Meaux Mustard Vinaigrette

Pan-Seared Yukon Gold Potatoes with Green Beans, Jicama, Red Onion Relish, and Parsley Dressing

Fennel and Watercress with Ratatouille, Smoked Shrimp, and Roasted Tomato Vinaigrette

Broccoli Bouquet with Garbanzo Bean and Tomato Relish, Spaghetti Squash, Chiffonade of Spinach, and Balsamic Vinaigrette

Spicy Garden Slaw with Leaf Lettuce, Toasted Peanuts, Crispy Corn Biscuits, and Cayenne Dressing

Romaine Lettuce, Granny Smith Apples, Toasted Hazelnuts, and New York State Cheddar Cheese with Sherry Wine Dressing

Bow Tie Pasta, Tangerines, Black Olives, and Grilled Red Onions with Olive Oil Dressing

Left: *Sliced Oranges and Grapefruit with Port-Soaked Currants and Raisins, Mini Dry Jack Cheese Fritters, and Citrus Vinaigrette*
Right: *Minted Melon and Fresh Berries with Toasted Cashews, Chive-Scented Cream Cheese, Cinnamon Brioche, and Late-Harvest Wine Dressing*

Arborio Rice Cakes with Marinated Plum Tomatoes, Artichokes, Sweet Peppers, and Charred Raw Tenderloin of Beef on a Bed of Leaf Spinach with Saffron Vinaigrette

Beets, Carrots, and Radishes Cut Japanese Style with Buckwheat Noodles, Screaming Peanuts, and Soy-Ginger Dressing

Panfried Black Turtle Bean Cakes with Avocado, Papaya, Strawberries, Jicama, Leaf Lettuce, and Peppered Honey-Lime Dressing

Mandarin Orange Basmati Rice with Sesame Stir-Fried Vegetables, Tangy Red Cabbage, and Szechuan Peppercorn Vinaigrette

Peppered Honey Peaches with Warm Pecan Cakes, "Bitter" Salad Greens, Turkey Scaloppine with Basil and Zinfandel, and Sour Mash Vinaigrette

Fruits

Roasted Root Vegetable Slaw with Gingered Apples, Raisins, and Walnuts, Apple and Rosemary-Scented Barley, and Brown Mustard Dressing

Serves 4

Gingered Apples, Raisins, and Walnuts

½ cup walnuts
1 cup port wine
1 teaspoon fresh lemon juice
1 Granny Smith apple, unpeeled
1 Red Delicious apple, unpeeled
1 tablespoon safflower oil

¾ cup finely diced onion
¼ cup finely diced celery
salt and freshly ground black pepper to taste
½ cup raisins
2 tablespoons cider vinegar
1 teaspoon grated fresh ginger

Brown Mustard Dressing

6 tablespoons spicy brown mustard
6 tablespoons pure apple juice
3 tablespoons mayonnaise

1½ tablespoons cider vinegar
salt and freshly ground black pepper to taste

Root Vegetable Slaw

1 medium rutabaga (about 1½ pounds),
  ends trimmed, peeled, and cut into sticks
  3 inches long and ⅛ inch thick
2 medium carrots (about ½ pound), ends
  trimmed, peeled, and cut into sticks
  3 inches long and ⅛ inch thick
4 tablespoons safflower oil
salt and freshly ground black pepper to taste

2 small turnips (about ½ pound), ends
  trimmed, peeled, and cut into sticks
  2 inches long and ⅛ inch thick
2 medium parsnips (about 6 ounces), ends
  trimmed, peeled, and cut into sticks
  3 inches long and ⅛ inch thick
Brown Mustard Dressing

Apple and Rosemary-Scented Barley

6 cups pure apple juice
1 teaspoon salt
1 teaspoon chopped fresh rosemary
1½ cups pearl barley

Salad Greens

¾ pound green leaf lettuce, cored, separated
   into leaves, washed, and dried

🦌

PREPARE THE GINGERED APPLES,
RAISINS, AND WALNUTS
Preheat the oven to 325 degrees Fahrenheit.

Toast the walnuts on a baking sheet in the preheated oven for 10 minutes. Cool the nuts to room temperature before chopping into ⅛-inch pieces. Set aside.

Heat the port wine in a 1½-quart saucepan over medium-high heat. Bring to a boil, then lower the heat and simmer for 15 minutes, until quite thick and reduced to about 2 tablespoons. Remove from the heat and set aside until needed.

In a 3-quart stainless steel bowl, add the lemon juice to 2 quarts of cold water. Core and quarter the apples, then slice each quarter widthwise into ¼-inch-thick slices. Immediately place the apple slices in the acidulated water to prevent them from discoloring.

Heat the safflower oil in a large nonstick sauté pan over medium heat. When the oil is hot, add the onion and celery. Season with salt and pepper, and cook, stirring occasionally, for 3 minutes. Drain the apples in a colander, rinse under cold water, and shake dry. Add the apples to the onion-celery mixture along with the raisins and cider vinegar. Continue to cook, stirring occasionally, for 2 minutes. Add the ginger, stir to combine, and cook for 1 minute.

Remove the pan from the heat, add the port wine reduction, and stir to combine. Add the walnuts and combine. Transfer the gingered apple mixture to a 3-quart stainless steel bowl; set aside, uncovered, at room temperature for up to 4 hours. Or cool to room temperature and then refrigerate in a covered, noncorrosive container for up to 4 days before serving.

MAKE THE BROWN MUSTARD DRESSING
In a 3-quart stainless steel bowl, whisk together until smooth the mustard, apple juice, mayonnaise, and cider vinegar. Season with salt and pepper and whisk to combine. Cover tightly with plastic wrap and refrigerate until needed.

MAKE THE ROOT VEGETABLE SLAW
Preheat the oven to 375 degrees Fahrenheit.

Place the rutabaga and carrot sticks in a 5-quart stainless steel bowl with 2 tablespoons of safflower oil. Season with salt and pepper, and stir to coat the vegetables with the oil. Transfer the rutabaga and carrot sticks to a nonstick baking sheet (spreading them in 1 layer over the surface of the pan) and set aside for a few minutes.

Repeat this process with the turnips and parsnips, using the remaining 2 tablespoons of safflower oil. Place the oil-coated turnips and parsnips on a separate baking sheet.

Place the baking sheets with the root vegetables in the preheated oven. Roast the carrots and parsnips for 10 minutes and the rutabagas and turnips for 15 minutes. Cool the vegetables at room temperature for 30 minutes. Transfer the root vegetables to a 7-quart stainless steel bowl. Add $1/2$ cup brown mustard dressing and use a rubber spatula to combine (cover the remaining $1/2$ cup with plastic wrap and refrigerate until needed). Cover the bowl tightly with plastic wrap and refrigerate the root vegetable slaw until needed (up to 2 days).

PREPARE THE APPLE AND ROSEMARY-SCENTED BARLEY
Heat the apple juice, salt, and rosemary in a 3-quart saucepan over medium-high heat. When the juice boils, add the barley. Return to a boil, then adjust the heat and simmer uncovered, stirring occasionally, for 45 minutes, until cooked but not mushy. Drain the barley in a large medium-gauge strainer, then cool with cold water. Transfer the barley to a 5-quart stainless steel bowl, cover with plastic wrap, and refrigerate until needed (up to 2 days).

ASSEMBLE THE SALAD
Divide and arrange the lettuce leaves on four 10- to 12-inch room-temperature plates. Arrange an equal amount of barley on the lettuce leaves. Use a kitchen spoon or rubber spatula to spread the barley into a ring toward the outside edge of each portion of let-

tuce. Dress each plate of lettuce and barley with 2 tablespoons of brown mustard dressing. Place an equal amount of root vegetable slaw inside each ring of barley, spreading the slaw to form a 2-inch-diameter well in the center of the slaw. Place an equal amount of gingered apples, raisins, and walnuts in each well of slaw. Serve immediately.

*S*piced Pork Burger Variation

1 tablespoon safflower oil	1 teaspoon celery seed
½ cup diced onion	2 tablespoons zinfandel or similar red wine
salt and freshly ground black pepper to taste	1 pound ground pork

Heat the safflower oil in a medium nonstick sauté pan over medium heat. When the oil is hot, add the onions, season with salt and pepper, and cook for 1 minute. Add the celery seed and cook for 2 more minutes, until the onions are tender. Add the red wine and cook for 30 seconds, until almost dry. Transfer the mixture to a dish and place, uncovered, in the refrigerator for 15 minutes to cool.

In a 5-quart stainless steel bowl, gently but thoroughly combine the chilled onion mixture with the ground pork. Gently form the mixture into four 4-ounce burgers 1 inch thick. Cover the burgers with plastic wrap and refrigerate until ready to cook (up to 24 hours).

Preheat the oven to 300 degrees Fahrenheit.

Season the burgers with salt and pepper.

Heat a large nonstick sauté pan over medium-high heat. When the pan is hot, sear the burgers for 2 minutes on each side, until browned. Transfer to a nonstick baking sheet and place in the preheated oven to finish cooking for 10 minutes. (The burgers may also be grilled over a medium wood or charcoal fire for about the same amount of time as listed for pan-searing.) Place a burger on top of each salad. Serve immediately.

Ale-Steamed Chicken Breast Variation

4 4-ounce boneless, skinless chicken breasts,
   each cut into 3 strips about 4 inches long
   and 1 inch wide
salt and freshly ground black pepper to taste

1 tablespoon safflower oil
½ cup thinly sliced onion
½ cup dark beer

Season the chicken strips with salt and pepper.

Heat the safflower oil in a large nonstick sauté pan over medium-high heat. When the oil is hot, place the chicken strips in the pan and brown on one side for 3 minutes. Turn the strips and add the onion and ale. Cover the pan with aluminum foil or tight-fitting lid and lower the heat to medium. Cook the chicken, covered, for 5 minutes. Remove from the heat. Use a slotted spoon to remove the chicken and onion from the pan and place an equal amount on each salad. Serve immediately.

The Chef's Touch

THE RAP on the root has been routed. For too long root vegetables suffered gastronomic inequity. In many homes, the unpleasant moans coming from the dinner table when the vegetable du jour was announced often gave way to even more disagreeable sounds, especially if that veggie happened to be of a subterranean class, such as parsnips, turnips, and rutabagas. Perhaps their unpopularity was because their names sounded odd, but more likely it was Mom or Dad's lack of fervor for cooking the root that passed down this legacy of vegetable phobia. Folks are finally realizing the explicit sweetness of these vegetables when they are handled with a little bit of care and creativity.

I know no better way to enhance the endemically sweet flavor of many root

(continued on next page)

The Chef's Touch

vegetables than oven-roasting. Unlike tomatoes, which are oven-roasted at a low temperature (200 to 225 degrees Fahrenheit), root vegetables must be roasted at about 375 degrees Fahrenheit or they will get tough. Cutting the vegetables in strips as described for this recipe shortens the roasting time to 10 to 15 minutes (larger cuts can be oven-roasted at the same temperature, with more time in the oven).

Try these oh-so-sweet oven-roasted root vegetables, and you may give up ice cream. And don't limit yourself to using the roasted Root Vegetable Slaw only with this salad; it is a particularly delicious accompaniment to grilled salmon or chicken.

While I'm on the subject of roots, here's a quick take on ginger. The edible part of the ginger plant is actually not a root but a rhizome (underground plant stems from which roots grow). Categorized as a spice, fresh ginger is another of nature's edible miracles. Slightly hot and startlingly sweet, ginger is easily overdone (use as directed or be prepared for palate shock). When selecting ginger, pick a smooth and hard rhizome. The freshest ginger will break clean with a snap.

The Brown Mustard Dressing recipe yields about 1 cup. The dressing may be stored in a covered, noncorrosive container in the refrigerator for 2 to 3 days.

I hope you are able to choose a pure apple juice for this recipe. The clean, sweet, and slightly tart flavor of the 100 percent pure apple juice produced from whole tree-ripened apples by the Murray Cider Company of Roanoke, Virginia, was instrumental in producing the exceptionally flavored barley for this recipe. If you are not able to locate Murray apple juice, be certain to pick a 100 percent pure apple juice.

Pearl barley, or pearled barley as it is sometimes listed, is an engaging grain that is easy to cook and very accepting of other flavors. In this recipe, the barley absorbs the apple flavor like a sponge and picks up a wonderful hint of rosemary.

One medium head of green leaf lettuce, about ¾ pound as purchased, should yield ½ pound of prepared lettuce. For crisp greens, spin-dry the washed leaves in a salad spinner.

The Chef's Touch

Some styles of zinfandel can overpower, so it is interesting that wine makers have taken note of the public's perception of zinfandel as a big, sometimes unwieldy wine and are now crafting blends that, although featuring "zin," include softer wines such as carignane and petite sirah. The Ridge Lytton Springs is a perfect example; it's a beauty, offering rich flavors and textures that please without overwhelming.

Pears and Caramelized Onions with Wheat Berries, Currants, Walnuts, and Basil-Parmesan Dressing

Serves 4

Basil-Parmesan Dressing

¼ cup walnuts
½ cup loosely packed basil leaves (½ ounce),
   stemmed, washed, and dried
½ ounce Parmesan cheese, grated

6 tablespoons extra-virgin olive oil
2 tablespoons red wine vinegar
1 tablespoon red raspberry vinegar
salt and freshly ground black pepper to taste

Wheat Berries and Currants

2 teaspoons salt
1½ cups wheat berries
½ cup walnuts
½ cup dried currants

2 tablespoons extra-virgin olive oil
2 tablespoons red raspberry vinegar
freshly ground black pepper to taste

Pears and Caramelized Onions

2 tablespoons extra-virgin olive oil
4 medium onions (about 1½ pounds),
   peeled and thinly sliced
salt and freshly ground black pepper to taste

1 teaspoon fresh lemon juice
4 medium pears (about 1½ pounds),
   unpeeled
½ cup water

Salad Greens

½ pound arugula, stemmed, washed, and
   dried

🦎

MAKE THE BASIL-PARMESAN DRESSING

Preheat the oven to 325 degrees Fahrenheit.

Toast the walnuts on a baking sheet in the preheated oven for 10 minutes. Remove the walnuts from the oven and cool to room temperature before using.

In the bowl of a food processor fitted with a metal blade, process the cooled walnuts, basil leaves, Parmesan cheese, and 2 tablespoons of olive oil for 15 seconds. Use a rubber spatula to scrape down the sides of the bowl, then process for 15 more seconds. Add the remaining 4 tablespoons of olive oil, red wine vinegar, and red raspberry vinegar, and process for 15 seconds. Transfer the dressing to a noncorrosive container. Season with salt and pepper, then cover with plastic wrap and refrigerate until needed.

PREPARE THE WHEAT BERRIES AND CURRANTS

Preheat the oven to 325 degrees Fahrenheit.

Bring 2 quarts of water with 2 teaspoons of salt to a boil in a 5-quart saucepan over high heat. When the water boils, add the wheat berries. Adjust the heat and simmer the wheat berries for 1 hour, until cooked but still quite crunchy.

While the wheat berries are cooking, toast the walnuts on a baking sheet in the preheated oven for 10 minutes. Remove the walnuts from the oven and cool to room temperature, then place them in the bowl of a food processor fitted with a metal blade and process for 10 seconds, until finely chopped. Set aside until needed.

Drain the cooked wheat berries in a colander, then transfer to a 5-quart stainless steel bowl. Add the currants, olive oil, and red raspberry vinegar, and stir to combine. Season with salt and pepper as needed. Cool the wheat berries at room temperature for 30 minutes before adding the finely chopped walnuts. Stir to combine. Set aside, uncovered, at room temperature for up to 2 hours or cover with plastic wrap and refrigerate for up to 24 hours before using.

Equipment

measuring cup
salad spinner
box grater
measuring spoons
paring knife
cook's knife
cutting board
baking sheet
food processor with metal
    blade
rubber spatula
plastic wrap
5-quart saucepan
colander
two 5-quart stainless steel
    bowls
large nonstick sauté pan
metal kitchen spoon
3-quart stainless steel bowl

Chicken variation requires:
tongs
slotted kitchen spoon

Venison variation requires:
medium nonstick sauté
    pan
slotted kitchen spoon

MAKE THE PEARS AND CARAMELIZED ONIONS

Heat the olive oil in a large nonstick sauté pan over medium heat. When the oil is hot, add the sliced onions and season lightly with salt and pepper. Cook the onions for 35 to 40 minutes, until a golden brown caramel color, stirring as necessary to prevent sticking and burning. While the onions are caramelizing, prepare the pears.

In a 3-quart stainless steel bowl, mix the lemon juice in 4 cups of cold water. Core and quarter the unpeeled pears. Slice each quarter lengthwise into ¼-inch-thick slices and immediately place in the acidulated water to prevent discoloration. Set aside until the onions are caramelized.

Add ½ cup of water to the caramelized onions, bring to a boil (this should take only 20 to 30 seconds), and then remove from the heat. Transfer the onions to a 5-quart stainless steel bowl. Drain the pears in a colander and then rinse under cold running water. Shake dry. Add the pears to the caramelized onions and stir gently (so as not to break the pears apart) to combine. Immediately cover the bowl with plastic wrap and set aside at room temperature for 10 minutes. The pears and caramelized onions may be used at this time, or kept, covered, at room temperature for up to 2 hours before serving.

ASSEMBLE THE SALAD

Place an equal amount of wheat berries and currants on each of four 10- to 12-inch room-temperature plates. Use a metal kitchen spoon or rubber spatula to spread the wheat berries into a ring near and around the outside edge of each plate. Place an equal amount of arugula leaves inside each ring of wheat berries. Dress the arugula and wheat berries with 2 tablespoons of dressing. Place an equal amount of the pear and caramelized onion mixture on each portion of arugula, then sprinkle each portion of pears and onions with 1 tablespoon of dressing. Serve immediately.

❦

*S*autéed Raspberry Chicken Variation

4 4-ounce boneless, skinless chicken breasts,
    cut the length of the breasts into strips
    ½ inch wide
salt and freshly ground black pepper to taste

1 tablespoon extra-virgin olive oil
1 tablespoon raspberry-flavored vinegar
½ pint fresh red raspberries

Season the chicken strips with salt and pepper.

Heat the olive oil in a large nonstick sauté pan over medium-high heat. When the oil is hot, add the chicken and sauté, turning as needed, about 5 minutes, until golden brown and cooked through. Add the vinegar and stir to combine. Remove from the heat, add the raspberries, and toss gently to combine. Use a slotted kitchen spoon to place an equal amount of chicken and raspberries on each salad. Serve immediately.

§

Pan-Seared Venison with Shallots and Port Variation

12 ounces venison loin meat, cut into
  $\frac{1}{2}$-ounce cubes
salt and freshly ground black pepper to taste

1 tablespoon safflower oil
3 tablespoons minced shallots
3 tablespoons port wine

Liberally season the venison with salt and pepper.

Heat the safflower oil in a medium nonstick sauté pan over high heat. When the oil is hot, add the venison meat and sear for 1 minute, turning to brown on all sides. Add the shallots and cook for 30 seconds. Add the port wine and cook, stirring often, for $2\frac{1}{2}$ minutes, until most of the port has evaporated. Remove from the heat and use a slotted spoon to place an equal amount of venison on each salad. Serve immediately.

The Chef's Touch

WHEN AWARD-WINNING cookbook author and food consultant Jeanne Jones called to ask me to be a guest chef at the fabled Canyon Ranch in Tucson, Arizona, I immediately accepted but remarked that inviting the author of *Death by Chocolate* to guest chef at this renowned health spa and resort would be akin to inviting Larry Flynt to preach to the choir. Jeanne, a

(continued on next page)

longtime food consultant for the Ranch, reminded me of a heart-healthy meal she enjoyed at The Trellis a couple of years earlier. She quipped that the chef responsible for it, albeit a chocolate lover, was well qualified to preach the gospel of low-fat foods because he had successfully lived with both sides of nutrition. So I became the inaugural chef for their guest chef series on heart-healthy cuisine.

While at Canyon Ranch, I spent a week working with executive chef John Luzader and his staff, reserving time to enjoy the amenities of this premier spa. Because of the success of *The Burger Meisters* cookbook, Chef Luzader was anxious to work with me on developing several vegetarian burgers. We experimented with making burgers out of a variety of beans, a combination of vegetables, and a multitude of starches, but my favorite burger contained wheat berries. Wheat berries, essentially whole wheat kernels, are flavorful and firm-textured grains that can be used in innumerable ways. Since that time they have found a place on our Garden Selections at The Trellis (these are authentically vegetarian entrees inspired by my first trip to Canyon Ranch—as a guest—in 1987) as well as on the regular menu. In fact, a featured item on our winter 1997 menu was a grilled chicken paillard with spicy carrots, wine-soaked raisins, toasted pine nuts, and curried wheat berries.

We purchase wheat berries for The Trellis from the wholesale division of Rice River Farms in Spooner, Wisconsin (see Sources, page 225). You may also be able to locate wheat berries at a health food store or supermarket with a bulk foods department.

To speed cooking time, soak the berries in cold water for 12 hours. After soaking, drain the berries, then cook for 24 minutes rather than an hour as listed in this recipe. I have found that this method delivers a cooked berry with a texture similar to that of the cooked berry as prepared in this recipe.

The Basil-Parmesan Dressing recipe yields ¾ cup. The dressing may be stored in a covered, noncorrosive container in the refrigerator for 2 to 3 days.

If the pears you purchase are hard and under-ripened, keep them at room temperature for 2 to 3 days before using. Once ripened, the pears may be refrigerated for several days without diminishing the flavor.

The Chef's Touch

Don't soak the pears in the acidulated water for more than 45 minutes (about the time it takes to caramelize the onions). Any longer, and the pears will become overly astringent.

Approximately ½ pound of arugula, as purchased, will yield ¼ pound of prepared arugula. If arugula is not available, consider substituting watercress or curly endive. For crisp greens, spin-dry the washed arugula in a salad spinner.

To add crunch to this salad, try garnishing each salad with toasted walnuts. An additional ½ cup of walnuts toasted along with the walnuts for the dressing would be a perfect amount.

My partner and friend John Curtis is responsible for selecting the wines for The Trellis. John has a wine lover's palate but consistently chooses delicious wines that we can offer at reasonable prices. One such selection was a recently released Chalk Hill Chardonnay, which John purchased prior to *Wine Spectator* magazine selecting it as one of the top California chardonnays. This chardonnay is abundant with flavor, filling your mouth with a lingering ripe fruit finish—a perfect match for this unusual salad.

Oven-Roasted Fruit with Curried Brown Rice, Belgian Endive, Crisp Apples, and Cherry Sake Dressing

Serves 4

Cherry Sake Dressing

¾ pound fresh red cherries, washed and
pitted (yielding about 2 cups)
1 cup water
¼ cup sake

1 tablespoon red raspberry vinegar
1 tablespoon fresh lemon juice
1 tablespoon granulated sugar

Oven-Roasted Fruit

1 medium pineapple (about 2 to 2½ pounds)
4 small plums (about 2 ounces each)

2 small peaches (about 3 ounces each)

Curried Brown Rice

3 tablespoons peanut oil
1 tablespoon curry powder
1 cup chopped scallions
1 cup brown rice

salt and freshly ground black pepper to taste
2 cups hot Vegetable Stock (see page 26)
¼ cup sake
1 cup sliced almonds

Salad Greens and Garnish

1 Granny Smith apple, unpeeled
1 Red Delicious apple, unpeeled
2 medium heads Belgian endive (about 3 to
4 ounces each)

½ pound watercress, trimmed, washed, and
dried

PREPARE THE CHERRY SAKE DRESSING

Combine the cherries, water, sake, vinegar, lemon juice, and sugar in a 3-quart saucepan. Bring to a boil, and continue to boil for 15 minutes, until the liquid is reduced by about half. Remove from the heat and transfer to a 1-quart stainless steel bowl. Cool the dressing in an ice and water bath to a temperature of 40 to 45 degrees Fahrenheit.

Transfer the cooled dressing to a food processor fitted with a metal blade and process the mixture until smooth, about 30 seconds. Return the dressing to the stainless steel bowl, cover with plastic wrap, and refrigerate until needed.

OVEN-ROAST THE FRUIT

Preheat the oven to 225 degrees Fahrenheit.

Line 2 baking sheets with parchment paper.

Peel, quarter, and core the pineapple. Cut each cored quarter widthwise into ¾-inch-thick pieces. Place the pineapple pieces, evenly spaced, on one of the parchment-lined baking sheets. Set aside.

Wash and then pit the plums and peaches. Cut each plum half into 2 pieces and each peach half into 3 pieces. Place the plum and peach pieces, cut side up and evenly spaced, on a parchment-lined baking sheet. Place the baking sheets on the top and center racks of the preheated oven and roast the fruit for 1½ hours, rotating the sheets from top to center halfway through the roasting time; at that time also turn each sheet 180 degrees. Remove the fruit from the oven and allow to cool to room temperature. Once cooled, the fruit should be covered with plastic wrap and refrigerated for up to 24 hours before using.

MAKE THE CURRIED BROWN RICE

Preheat the oven to 350 degrees Fahrenheit.

Heat 2 tablespoons of peanut oil in a 5-quart saucepan over medium-high heat. When the oil is hot, add the curry powder

Equipment

cherry pitter
measuring cups
measuring spoons
cook's knife
cutting board
lettuce spinner
3-quart saucepan
1-quart stainless steel bowl
instant-read test
    thermometer
food processor with metal
    blade
plastic wrap
2 baking sheets
parchment paper
5-quart saucepan with
    cover
kitchen spoon
two 5-quart stainless steel
    bowls
rubber spatula

Lamb variation requires:
large nonstick sauté pan
colander
slotted kitchen spoon

*Sea scallop variation
    requires:*
3-quart stainless steel bowl
paper towels
colander
large nonstick sauté pan
slotted kitchen spoon

and cook, stirring constantly, for 1 minute. Add the scallions and cook for 1 minute. Add the brown rice, season with salt and pepper, and stir to coat the rice with the oil. Add the hot vegetable stock and stir to incorporate. Cover the saucepan and place in the preheated oven for 1 hour. Remove from the oven and immediately transfer the rice to a 5-quart stainless steel bowl. In a small bowl, whisk the sake and 1 tablespoon of peanut oil together. Add this mixture to the rice and use a fork to stir and incorporate it into the rice. Cool the rice to room temperature, stirring occasionally.

When the rice has cooled to room temperature, add the almonds, and stir to combine. Place the rice in the refrigerator to chill completely, about 1 hour.

FINISH AND ASSEMBLE THE SALAD

Core and quarter the unpeeled apples. Cut into ¼-inch dice. Place the apples in a 5-quart stainless steel bowl. Whisk the cherry sake dressing. Pour ¼ cup of dressing over the apples and use a rubber spatula to combine until the apples are thoroughly coated with the dressing. Set aside while preparing the endives.

Cut each endive in half lengthwise. Cut the core out from each half. Cut each half into ¼-inch-thick strips the length of the endive. Gently wash and dry the endives (rough handling will cause them to discolor). Add the endives to the bowl with the apples. Pour ¼ cup of dressing over the endives. Use a rubber spatula to gently combine them with the apples and coat with the dressing.

Divide and arrange the watercress, stem ends toward the center, in a ring with the leaf ends near the outside edge of four 10- to 12-inch room-temperature plates. Divide and arrange the endive and apple mixture in a ring over the stem ends of the watercress. Place an equal amount of rice inside the ring of endives and apples. Arrange an equal amount of each of the oven-roasted fruit on each portion of rice. Whisk the dressing. Sprinkle each salad with 2 to 3 tablespoons of the dressing. Serve immediately.

%

"Almost Hotter Than Hell" Lamb with Jicama and Anaheim Peppers Variation

1 teaspoon curry powder
1 teaspoon dry mustard
¼ teaspoon cracked black pepper
¼ teaspoon ground cardamom
¼ teaspoon cayenne pepper
¼ teaspoon ground cumin
¼ teaspoon salt
⅛ teaspoon ground allspice
1 pound well-trimmed lamb meat, cut into
  1-inch pieces

1 tablespoon peanut oil
¼ pound jicama, peeled and cut into strips
  1½ inches long and ¼ inch thick
1 medium Anaheim chili pepper (about
  3 ounces), cut in half lengthwise, core
  removed, seeded, membrane removed,
  and cut into strips 1 inch long and ⅛ inch
  wide
¼ cup sake

Thoroughly combine the spices in a 5-quart stainless steel bowl. Add the lamb pieces and coat evenly and completely.

Heat the peanut oil in a large nonstick sauté pan over medium-high heat. When the oil is hot, add the lamb and sauté it for about 3 minutes for medium-rare or longer if you prefer more well done and less juicy meat. Add the jicama and pepper, and stir gently to combine. Add the sake, stir gently to combine, and remove the pan from the heat. Drain the meat mixture in a colander, then use a slotted kitchen spoon to place an equal amount on each salad.

🦎

*P*an-Seared Maple-and-Ginger-Coated
Sea Scallops Variation

2 tablespoons pure maple syrup
½ teaspoon ground ginger
1 pound sea scallops, side muscle removed

salt to taste
2 tablespoons finely chopped scallions
1 tablespoon finely minced ginger

In a 3-quart stainless steel bowl, whisk together the maple syrup and ginger.

Pat the scallops dry with paper towels. Lightly season the scallops with salt. Add the scallops to the maple syrup and use a rubber spatula to combine and thoroughly coat the scallops with the syrup. Transfer the scallops to a colander and drain while heating the pan.

Heat a large nonstick sauté pan over high heat. When the pan is *very hot,* add the drained scallops and cook for about 1½ minutes (or longer if well-done and rubbery scallops are preferred). Remove the pan from the heat. Add the scallions and ginger, and stir to combine. Use a slotted kitchen spoon to place an equal amount on each salad.

The Chef's Touch

As I mentioned in "Salad Days at Ganache Hill," most recipes in this book were tested during January to March 1997. However, because of unforeseen circumstances, I took a short hiatus, then finished recipe testing for *Salad Days* in June 1997. I mention this because this particular salad originally had a dressing made with pomegranate seeds rather than fresh cherries. During the late spring testing, we scoured the globe for pomegranates without any luck, since their primary availability is late fall and early winter. Even though I contended that "they must be growing somewhere in the universe at any given time," no pomegranates were found. When Trellis assistant chef Brett Bailey joined me in June to finish the recipe testing, he suggested we craft a dressing with the luscious-looking cherries he had recently seen at a local market. Bravo, Brett!

The Chef's Touch

The Cherry Sake Dressing recipe yields about 2 cups. You can store the dressing in a covered, noncorrosive container in the refrigerator for 2 to 3 days, then whisk before using.

Handle the Belgian endives with care because the leaves will discolor when bruised. Gently wash and then pat them dry before using.

One large bunch of watercress, about ½ pound as purchased, should yield ¼ pound of trimmed (cut away about ½ inch of the stem ends), washed, and dried leaves. For crisp greens, spin-dry the watercress in a lettuce spinner.

Although I strive to purchase virtually every ingredient used in this cookbook at local markets, I confess that when it comes to sea scallops, I would not dream of cooking most scallops available to the general public. I know of no other seafood that is as systematically abused as sea scallops. Routinely "dipped" in a chemical treatment that whitens the scallops, extends shelf life, and pumps up the weight, these scallops cook up tasteless and dry—the antithesis of the unadulterated but succulent "sticky" scallops that we buy and serve at The Trellis. Make it a point to query the manager or market owner about whether the scallops have been chemically treated. If the scallops have been "dipped," they will not stick to each other and will have a wet, soapy appearance.

To ensure lovely and delicious scallops, make sure the pan is "smokin'" hot before adding the scallops. If you do not have a forceful ventilation system that can handle the smoke, however, I suggest you cook them over moderate heat. The scallops will not appear caramelized as they do from the "smokin'" pan, but they will still be divine.

I love oven-roasted fruit. The roasting exponentially elicits the sweetness and complex flavors of the fruit. Rather than pairing this with a wine that competes with the sweetness of the fruit, I recommend a red Bordeaux that is flush with spice, pleases with velvety tannins, and treats the palate to a suave finish. Of the many Bordeaux wines that fit the bill, I suggest almost any vintage of the noteworthy and moderately priced Château Prieure-Lichine, Margaux.

Peppered Honey Peaches with Warm Pecan Cakes, "Bitter" Salad Greens, and Sour Mash Vinaigrette

Serves 4

Sour Mash Vinaigrette

1½ tablespoons cider vinegar
  1 tablespoon sour mash whiskey
  2 tablespoons walnut oil

  6 tablespoons safflower oil
salt and freshly ground black pepper to taste

Peppered Honey Peaches

8 small peaches (about 3 ounces each)
3 tablespoons sour mash whiskey

3 tablespoons honey
2 teaspoons freshly cracked black pepper

Warm Pecan Cakes

¾ cup pecans
  1 cup yellow cornmeal
½ teaspoon salt
¾ cup apple cider

½ cup buttermilk
  2 teaspoons pure maple syrup
  1 large egg
1½ teaspoons safflower oil

Salad Greens

¼ pound arugula, stemmed, washed, and dried
¼ pound dandelion, stemmed, washed, and dried

½ pound watercress, trimmed, washed, and dried

MAKE THE SOUR MASH VINAIGRETTE

Whisk together in a 3-quart stainless steel bowl the vinegar and whiskey. Add the walnut oil and then the safflower oil in a slow, steady stream while whisking until incorporated. Season with salt and pepper, and whisk to combine. Cover with plastic wrap and set aside at room temperature until needed.

PREPARE THE PEPPERED HONEY PEACHES

Wash and pit the peaches. Cut each pitted peach half lengthwise into 6 sections. Set aside.

Heat the whiskey to a boil in a medium nonstick sauté pan over medium heat, then add the honey and stir to combine. Heat the mixture for exactly 2 minutes, then immediately remove from the heat. Add the peach sections. Sprinkle the pepper over the peaches. Use a rubber spatula to gently coat the peaches with the honey-whiskey mixture. Transfer the peaches to a 3-quart stainless steel bowl, cover with plastic wrap, and set aside at room temperature for up to 3 hours before serving.(Once cooled to room temperature, the peaches may be refrigerated for up to 12 hours before serving.)

MAKE THE PECAN CAKES AND ASSEMBLE THE SALAD

Preheat the oven to 325 degrees Fahrenheit.

Toast the pecans on a baking sheet in the preheated oven for 8 minutes. Remove the pecans from the oven and cool to room temperature. Process the pecans in the bowl of a food processor fitted with a metal blade until finely chopped, about 10 to 12 seconds (or finely chop the pecans by hand using a cook's knife).

Combine in a 5-quart stainless steel bowl the cornmeal, chopped pecans, and salt. Set aside.

Heat the cider and buttermilk in a 1½-quart saucepan over medium-high heat. When hot, pour the cider mixture into the

Equipment
measuring spoons
measuring cups
cook's knife
cutting board
lettuce spinner
two 3-quart stainless steel bowls
whisk
plastic wrap
medium nonstick sauté pan
rubber spatula
baking sheet
food processor with metal blade
5-quart stainless steel bowl
1½-quart saucepan
7-quart stainless steel bowl
slotted kitchen spoon
large nonstick sauté pan
spatula
Turkey variation requires:
meat cleaver
tongs
Soft-shell crab variation requires:
kitchen scissors
parchment paper
paper towels
pie tin

bowl of dry ingredients. Add the maple syrup and then use a whisk to stir the mixture until thoroughly blended. Set aside for 5 minutes.

Gently whisk the egg in a small bowl. Add the egg to the pecan cake batter and stir to combine. Cover the bowl with plastic wrap and set aside while assembling the salads.

Combine the arugula, dandelion, and watercress in a 7-quart stainless steel bowl. Vigorously whisk the vinaigrette. Add the vinaigrette to the greens and gently toss until the leaves are coated with the vinaigrette. Divide and arrange the greens on four 10- to 12-inch room-temperature plates. Use a slotted spoon to place an equal amount of the peppered honey peaches in the center of each portion of greens. (Reserve the liquid to drizzle on the warm pecan cakes.) Set the plates aside while cooking the pecan cakes.

Heat a large nonstick sauté pan over medium heat. When the pan is hot, lightly coat the cooking surface with ½ teaspoon of safflower oil and then wipe dry. Place 6 individual tablespoons of the batter in the hot pan, evenly spaced, and cook for 1½ minutes, until light brown around the edges. Turn these silver-dollar-sized cakes and cook for 1½ more minutes. Transfer the hot cakes to a warm baking sheet or platter and set aside while preparing the remaining cakes. Repeat the cooking procedure with the remaining 1 teaspoon of safflower oil and batter. There should be enough batter to prepare 10 more cakes.

Place 4 warm pecan cakes on each salad. Drizzle a small amount of the reserved liquid from the peppered honey peaches on each pecan cake and serve immediately.

Turkey Scaloppine with Basil and Zinfandel Variation

1 pound boneless, skinless white turkey meat
salt and freshly ground black pepper to taste

16 small fresh basil leaves
1 teaspoon extra-virgin olive oil
¼ cup red zinfandel

Slicing across the grain, cut the turkey into 16 pieces that are 1 ounce each. Season the turkey pieces on both sides with salt and pepper. Place the turkey pieces, one at a time, on a sheet of plastic wrap. Place a basil leaf on each piece of turkey. Cover with plastic wrap and then use a meat cleaver or the bottom of a sauté pan to slightly flatten the turkey. Remove and discard the plastic wrap and set aside the turkey; the basil leaf will adhere to the flattened turkey. Repeat until all the turkey pieces have been flattened into scaloppine.

Brush the bottom of a large nonstick sauté pan with ½ teaspoon of olive oil. Heat the pan over medium-high heat. When the pan is hot, place 8 turkey scaloppine in the pan, basil leaf side down, and cook for 45 seconds. Use tongs to turn the scaloppine and cook for another 45 seconds. Transfer to a warm platter and set aside. Repeat the cooking procedure with the remaining turkey (wipe the pan clean before brushing with the remaining oil). After removing the second batch of turkey scaloppine from the pan, immediately add the zinfandel wine to the pan. Cook the wine over medium-high heat for about 30 seconds. Sprinkle the wine over the turkey scaloppine. Place 4 slices of turkey on each salad and serve immediately.

*

*P*ecan-Crusted Soft-Shell Crab Variation

4 live large soft-shell crabs	salt and freshly ground black pepper to taste
½ cup buttermilk	½ cup pecans
2 tablespoons sour mash whiskey	½ cup all-purpose flour
1 large egg	4 tablespoons safflower oil

Rinse the live crabs, one at a time, under cool running water to remove unwanted debris such as seaweed or other packing material. Cutting straight across the face using a pair of scissors or a cook's knife, remove the eye-and-mouth section of the crab. Place the crab on its back on a clean, dry surface covered with a piece of parchment paper or plastic wrap that will keep the surface clean and dry. Gently press down on the center portion of the crab to remove the yellow bile. Pull away and cut off the apron (this flap on the bottom of the crab looks like a **T** on the male crabs and a **V** on the female crabs). Turn the crab right side up. Lift up the soft shell flap on each end and pull out the spongy gill tissue. Rinse the dressed crabs, one at a time, under cool running water and gently pat dry with paper towels. Set the crabs aside for a few minutes while preparing the marinade, or the dressed crabs may be covered with plastic wrap and refrigerated for up to 24 hours before cooking.

In a 3-quart stainless steel bowl, whisk together the buttermilk, whiskey, and egg. Season the crabs with salt and pepper, then submerge them in the marinade. Cover the bowl with plastic wrap and refrigerate while preparing the pecan coating.

Preheat the oven to 325 degrees Fahrenheit.

Toast the pecans on a baking sheet in the preheated oven for 5 minutes, then cool the nuts to room temperature. Place the cooled pecans and flour in the bowl of a food processor fitted with a metal blade and process for 20 seconds. Transfer the pecan coating to a pie tin.

Remove the crabs from the marinade. Place the crabs, one at a time, in the pecan coating and coat evenly and thoroughly. Set aside.

Heat the safflower oil in a large nonstick sauté pan over medium-high heat. When the oil is hot, place the crabs in the pan, belly side up. Cook the crabs for $2\frac{1}{2}$ to 3 minutes on each side, until uniformly brown. Transfer the crabs to a paper-towel-lined platter to drain for a few minutes. Place a crab on top of each salad and serve immediately.

The Chef's Touch

E U G E N E   W A L T E R wrote in his introduction to *American Cooking: Southern Style* that the best of indigenous southern cooking existed mostly in homes and not in restaurants. The year was 1971, and restaurants like Canoe in Atlanta, Elizabeth on 37th in Savannah, Mark's Place in Miami, Louis' Charleston Grill in Charleston, Magnolia Grill in Durham, and the Highlands Bar & Grill in Birmingham, just to name a few, did not exist. I would argue that today those restaurants are where the very best of both classic and neoclassic southern cooking is taking place. To me, this salad recipe incorporates both ingredients that are southern and the spirit of the new cuisine of the South.

The Sour Mash Vinaigrette recipe yields ⅔ cup. The vinaigrette may be kept at room temperature for 3 to 4 hours before using or refrigerated in a covered, noncorrosive container for 3 to 4 days. If refrigerated, return the vinaigrette to room temperature and whisk vigorously before using.

Sour mash whiskey is not made just for "sippin'." Its depth and character of flavor also make it suitable as an exciting flavor boost to a range of foods, from ice creams to salad dressings. Use it as a marinade for fish or poultry, sprinkle it over fresh fruit just before serving, add it to a batch of homemade ice cream, or make the sour mash vinaigrette. Wherever you use it, prepare to have your taste buds titillated and always save a wee bit for "sippin'."

If you chill the Peppered Honey Peaches in the refrigerator for more than the recommended 12 hours, they will begin to lose much of their texture. For my palate it's worth the effort to prepare the peaches within 2 to 3 hours of serving and serve them at room temperature rather than refrigerating them. If you must refrigerate the peaches for the sake of organization, bring them to room temperature beforehand to enhance their flavor.

I have a pair of forty-foot-tall pecan trees directly outside my office window at Ganache Hill. Previously, I allowed the squirrels to harvest the nuts, but this year I plan on denying my frenetic little friends their treat and will gather the nuts myself. (Wish me luck.) While I am on the subject of one of my favorite nuts, I suggest that when you toast the pecans for the Warm Pecan Cakes, you toast an extra ½ cup and sprinkle these over the salad for some tasty crunch.

Approximately ¼ pound of arugula and ¼ pound of dandelion will yield ⅛ pound of each prepared green for this salad. One large bunch of watercress, about ½ pound, should yield ¼ pound of trimmed (cut away about ½ inch of the stem ends), washed, and dried leaves. For crisp greens, separately spin-dry the washed arugula, dandelion, and watercress in a lettuce spinner.

If you have never cooked turkey in the fashion described for the scaloppine, you are in for a treat. The meat, when quickly pan-seared as recommended, is as tender as veal.

Although I much prefer fresh soft-shell crabs, excellent quality frozen soft-shell crabs are available year-round. If you do purchase frozen crabs, thaw them in the refrigerator and handle with care, because after being frozen, the claws have a tendency to separate from the body of the crab.

Shepherd Rouse has carved out a niche as arguably the best wine maker in Virginia. You will find no argument with his Rockbridge Pinot Noir, bursting with ripe fruit flavor and distinguished by its graceful finish. This wine will complete your southern exposure.

Minted Melon and Fresh Berries with Toasted Cashews, Chive-Scented Cream Cheese, Cinnamon Brioche, and Late-Harvest Wine Dressing

Serves 4

Cinnamon Brioche

2 cups all-purpose flour
1 teaspoon salt
½ teaspoon ground cinnamon
2 large eggs
1 tablespoon granulated sugar

¼ cup warm water
1 tablespoon active dry yeast
6 tablespoons plus 1 teaspoon unsalted butter, softened

Late-Harvest Wine Dressing

½ cup late-harvest wine
2 tablespoons honey

2 teaspoons fresh lemon juice
1 teaspoon cornstarch

Minted Melon

½ cup orange-flavored vodka
½ cup fresh orange juice
1 tablespoon minced orange zest
1 tablespoon granulated sugar

1 small ripe melon (about 2¼ to 2½ pounds), peeled, seeded, and cut into 1-inch chunks
1 tablespoon finely sliced fresh mint

Chive-Scented Cream Cheese

¼ pound boursin cheese
¼ pound cream cheese, softened

1 tablespoon chopped fresh chives

Salad Greens and Garnish

³/₄ cup cashews

 1 pound Boston lettuce, cored, separated
   into leaves, washed, and dried

 1 cup sliced (¹/₄ inch thick) fresh strawberries

¹/₂ cup fresh blackberries, picked through and
   rinsed

¹/₂ cup fresh blueberries, picked through and
   rinsed

¹/₂ cup fresh raspberries

 8 pretty sprigs fresh mint to garnish

Equipment

measuring cups
measuring spoons
cook's knife
cutting board
vegetable peeler
lettuce spinner
sifter
wax paper
1-quart stainless steel bowl
whisk
electric mixer with dough
  hook and paddle
rubber spatula
5-quart stainless steel bowl
100 percent cotton towel
pie tin
plastic wrap
pastry brush
9- by 5- by 3-inch loaf pan
rolling pin
1¹/₂-quart saucepan
7-quart stainless steel bowl
baking sheet
serrated slicer
spatula
slotted kitchen spoon

Chicken variation requires:
large nonstick sauté pan
tongs
thin-bladed stainless steel
  knife or lemon stripper

Shrimp variation requires:
large sauté pan with cover
colander

🦎

PREPARE THE CINNAMON BRIOCHE

Sift the flour onto a large piece of wax paper. Remeasure 2 cups of sifted flour. (There will be slightly more sifted flour than the necessary 2 cups; reserve the remainder for later use.) Sift the remeasured 2 cups of flour with the salt and cinnamon onto a large sheet of wax paper and set aside.

In a small bowl, whisk the eggs together.

In the bowl of an electric mixer, dissolve the sugar in the warm water. Add the yeast and stir gently to dissolve. Allow the mixture to stand and foam for 2 to 3 minutes.

Add the sifted flour mixture and the whisked eggs to the dissolved sugar and yeast. Combine on the low speed of an electric mixer fitted with a dough hook for 1 minute. Use a rubber spatula to scrape down the sides of the bowl, then continue to mix on low speed until the dough begins to form a ball, about 2 minutes. Scrape down the sides of the bowl and pull the dough off the hook. Adjust the mixer speed to medium-low and add the 6 tablespoons of softened butter, 2 tablespoons at a time, being certain that the butter is thoroughly incorporated before adding the next 2 tablespoons. (When most of the dough attaches itself to the dough hook, stop the mixer and pull the dough off the hook.) Continue to add the butter until all 6 tablespoons have been incorporated in the dough, about 12 minutes.

Remove the dough from the mixer and form it into a smooth ball. Place the brioche dough ball in a stainless steel bowl, cover with a dry towel, place in a warm location, and allow to rise until the dough has doubled in volume, about 1 hour (depending on the warmth of the space). Punch down the dough to its original size, transfer to a pie tin, then flatten the dough to cover the inside of the pie tin. Cover with plastic wrap and place in the freezer for 15 minutes.

Coat the bottom and sides of a 9- by 5- by 3-inch loaf pan with the remaining 1 teaspoon of butter. Set aside.

Remove the dough from the freezer and place on a clean, dry, lightly floured work surface. Roll the dough into a rectangle measuring 9 by 15 inches. (Use the reserved flour to dust the work surface and rolling pin as necessary to prevent the dough from sticking.) Starting with one short side, use your hands to roll the dough into a spiral and place in the prepared loaf pan. Cover the pan with a dry towel and place in a warm location so the dough can rise until it has almost doubled in volume, about 1½ hours. (Again, this may take longer if your kitchen is very cool.)

Preheat the oven to 325 degrees Fahrenheit.

Bake the brioche in the preheated oven for 30 minutes, until golden brown. Cool the baked brioche in the loaf pan for 15 minutes. Remove the loaf from the pan and cool to room temperature before slicing.

MAKE THE LATE-HARVEST WINE DRESSING

Heat the late-harvest wine and honey to a boil in a 1½-quart saucepan over medium-high heat. While the wine mixture is heating, whisk together the lemon juice and cornstarch in a small bowl until combined and smooth. When the wine mixture begins to boil, add the cornstarch mixture and whisk to combine. Boil for 30 seconds, whisking constantly until slightly syrupy. Transfer the dressing to a 1-quart stainless steel bowl and cool in an ice and water bath until thoroughly chilled. Cover with plastic wrap and refrigerate until needed.

MAKE THE MINTED MELON

In a 7-quart stainless steel bowl, whisk together the vodka, orange juice, orange zest, and granulated sugar. Add the melon and sliced mint and use a rubber spatula to combine the ingredients. Cover the bowl with plastic wrap and set aside at room temperature for 1 hour (and up to 3 hours). While the melon is macerating, prepare the cream cheese.

PREPARE THE CHIVE-SCENTED CREAM CHEESE

Place the boursin cheese and cream cheese in the bowl of an electric mixer fitted with a paddle. Beat on high speed for 1 minute, until smooth and thoroughly combined.

Add the chives and beat on high for 4 to 5 seconds, until combined. Cover the cheese with plastic wrap and set aside at room temperature while finishing the preparations to assemble the salads.

FINISH AND ASSEMBLE THE SALAD
Preheat the oven to 325 degrees Fahrenheit.

Toast the cashews on a baking sheet in the preheated oven for 20 minutes, until uniformly golden brown. Remove the cashews from the oven and cool to room temperature. (Keep the oven hot to toast the brioche.)

Slice the brioche loaf into 16 slices ½ inch thick. Trim the crust away from each slice of brioche. Toast the brioche slices on a baking sheet in the preheated oven for 12 minutes, until golden brown. Turn the slices over and toast for an additional 3 minutes. Remove the brioche toast from the oven and the baking sheet. Cool for 2 to 3 minutes.

Spread 1 ounce of the chive-scented cream cheese on 8 slices of toasted brioche. Top these slices of brioche with another slice of toasted brioche. Cut each brioche "sandwich" in half.

Divide and arrange the lettuce leaves on four 10- to 12-inch room-temperature plates. Stir the late-harvest wine dressing, then drizzle 1 tablespoon over each portion of lettuce. Add the berries to the minted melon and use a rubber spatula to gently but thoroughly combine. Use a slotted spoon to place an equal amount of the melon and berries on the center of each portion of greens. Drizzle 1 tablespoon of dressing over each portion of melon and berries.

Sprinkle the toasted cashews over the fruit. Arrange 4 brioche sandwich halves on each plate. Garnish each salad with a sprig of mint. Serve immediately.

*M*artini Chicken with a Twist Variation

4 4- to 5-ounce boneless, skinless chicken breasts, cut the length of the breasts into strips ½ inch wide
salt and freshly ground black pepper to taste
½ teaspoon safflower oil
½ cup gin

¼ cup dry vermouth
2 tablespoons fresh lemon juice
12 lemon twists (2- to 2½-inch-long strips of lemon peel, ¼ inch wide; see page 221 in Techniques)

Season the chicken strips with salt and pepper.

Heat a large nonstick sauté pan over medium-high heat. When the pan is hot, lightly coat the cooking surface with safflower oil and then wipe dry. Place the chicken strips in the hot pan and sauté, turning as needed, about 3 minutes, until light brown. Transfer the chicken to a 5-quart stainless steel bowl. Add the gin, vermouth, lemon juice, and lemon twists to the sauté pan and simmer for 1½ minutes. Pour the liquid and twists over the chicken. Cover the bowl with plastic wrap and set aside at room temperature for 15 minutes. Remove the plastic wrap and cool the chicken in the liquid to room temperature. Once cooled to room temperature, the chicken may be used, or remove the cooled chicken and lemon twists from the liquid, cover with plastic wrap, and then refrigerate for up to 24 hours before serving. To serve, place an equal amount of chicken strips and lemon twists on each salad.

※

*L*emon and Marjoram Shrimp Variation

1 cup Riesling or other slightly sweet white wine
½ cup lemon juice
½ cup water
1 tablespoon minced lemon zest
1 tablespoon chopped fresh marjoram
1 teaspoon salt
¼ teaspoon cracked black peppercorns
1 pound large shrimp, peeled and deveined

Heat the Riesling, lemon juice, water, lemon zest, marjoram, salt, and peppercorns in a large sauté pan over medium-high heat. Bring the liquid to a boil, then add the shrimp and cook for 1 minute before removing the pan from the heat. Immediately place a cover over the pan and allow to stand for 5 minutes.

Drain the shrimp in a colander. Bring the shrimp to room temperature before placing an equal amount on each salad. The shrimp may also be refrigerated after reaching room temperature but serve chilled within 24 hours.

The Chef's Touch

PUT YOUR trepidations about making brioche aside. This recipe easily delivers a perfectly delicious and buttery loaf of brioche every time. As this recipe proves, you don't need to bake brioche in a conventional fluted form; however, for best results, prepare the brioche using a table model electric mixer. If you do not have this piece of equipment, I suggest you purchase a loaf of brioche or another rich yeast-raised bread such as the traditional Jewish challah to make your sandwiches.

I used a 1995 Virginia-produced Rockbridge V d'Or to make the Late-Harvest Wine Dressing. This award-winning wine is made from late-harvest Vidal Blanc grapes that are pressed frozen. It may seem a shame to make a salad dressing from such an outstanding wine, but because the ingredients in this dressing are so straightforward, the key ingredient—the late-harvest wine— needs a clear, crisp flavor that stands out on the palate rather than weighing it down with a cloying sweetness.

The Late-Harvest Wine Dressing recipe yields ⅔ cup. The dressing may be stored in a covered, noncorrosive container in the refrigerator for several days.

For this salad we used a small cantaloupe (2¼ to 2½ pounds), which yielded 4 cups of peeled and seeded 1-inch chunks. Other commonly available melons such as honeydew or crenshaw may be used, although they may yield more fruit than you need.

With several hundred different varieties of mint, spearmint and peppermint usually are the culinary mints of choice. At Ganache Hill my iconoclastic herb garden grows only orange mint and catmint. The orange variety has a subtler and more versatile flavor, which I prefer over the more assertive spearmint or peppermint for this salad. Although catmint is strictly ornamental, it's worth growing for the spectacular spiky purple flowers that stand out in the garden.

You may substitute gin for the vodka or omit the booze altogether and double up on the orange juice.

One large head of Boston lettuce, about 1 pound as purchased, should yield ½ pound of prepared lettuce. For crisp greens, spin-dry the washed leaves in a salad spinner.

Be sure to wash all the berries (except the raspberries) gently but well, with a thorough spraying of warm water, then pat them dry with paper towels.

A sparkling wine from California would make a delightful beverage with this salad. Choose a smooth, vivaciously fruity wine like the Iron Horse Brut Rosé, and stars will shine no matter the time of day.

Sliced Oranges and Grapefruit with Port-Soaked Currants and Raisins, Mini Dry Jack Cheese Fritters, and Citrus Vinaigrette

Serves 4

Port-Soaked Currants and Raisins

½ cup currants
½ cup raisins

½ cup port wine

Citrus Vinaigrette

2 tablespoons fresh orange juice
2 tablespoons port wine
1 tablespoon cider vinegar
½ tablespoon honey

½ teaspoon finely minced orange zest
¼ cup extra-virgin olive oil
¼ cup safflower oil
salt and freshly ground black pepper to taste

Mini Dry Jack Cheese Fritters

½ cup walnuts
1 cup all-purpose flour
1 teaspoon baking powder
¼ teaspoon salt
¼ teaspoon cream of tartar

2 ounces grated Dry Jack cheese
¼ cup Budweiser beer
¼ cup whole milk
1 large egg
6 cups peanut oil

Salad Greens and Garnish

4 medium pink grapefruit (about 14 ounces
   each), peeled and cut into slices ¼ inch
   thick
4 large navel oranges (about 8 ounces each),
   peeled and cut into slices ¼ inch thick
¾ pound curly endive, cored, trimmed, cut
   into ¾-inch pieces, washed, and dried
24 Belgian endive leaves, washed and dried

ॐ

SOAK THE CURRANTS AND RAISINS
Combine the currants and raisins together in a 1-quart stainless steel bowl.

Heat the port wine in a 1½-quart saucepan over medium-
high heat. When the wine begins to simmer, remove from the
heat and pour over the raisins and currants. Cover the bowl
with plastic wrap and set aside at room temperature for 12
hours.

MAKE THE CITRUS VINAIGRETTE
Whisk together in a 3-quart stainless steel bowl the orange
juice, port wine, cider vinegar, honey, and orange zest. Add the
olive oil and safflower oil in a slow, steady stream while whisking until incorporated. Season with salt and pepper. Cover with
plastic wrap and set aside at room temperature until needed.

PREPARE THE FRITTERS
Preheat the oven to 325 degrees Fahrenheit.

Toast the walnuts on a baking sheet in the preheated oven
for 10 minutes. Remove the walnuts from the oven and cool to
room temperature before using a cook's knife to chop them
into ⅛-inch pieces.

Combine the toasted walnuts, flour, baking powder, salt, and
cream of tartar in the bowl of an electric mixer fitted with a
paddle. Mix on low speed for 30 seconds to combine. Add the

Equipment

measuring cups
measuring spoons
vegetable peeler
cook's knife
cutting board
box grater
sharp serrated knife
lettuce spinner
two 1-quart stainless steel
   bowls
1½-quart saucepan
plastic wrap
3-quart stainless steel bowl
whisk
baking sheet
electric mixer with paddle
rubber spatula
deep fat fryer or heavy-
   duty 4- to 5-quart
   saucepan
candy/deep-frying
   thermometer
metal tongs or slotted
   spoon
paper towels

Beef variation requires:
medium nonstick sauté
   pan
pie tin
thin-bladed sharp knife
spatula

Shad roe variation requires:
large nonstick sauté pan
spatula
nonstick baking sheet

Dry Jack cheese and mix on low for 30 seconds. In a small bowl, whisk together the beer, milk, and egg, then add to the mixing bowl and mix on low for 30 seconds. Stop the mixer and scrape down the sides of the bowl with a rubber spatula. Increase the mixer speed to medium and mix for 30 more seconds, just until blended.

Preheat the oven to 200 degrees Fahrenheit.

Heat the peanut oil in a deep-fryer (or high-sided heavy-duty saucepan) to 350 degrees Fahrenheit. When the oil has reached that temperature, use a tablespoon measure to portion the batter and drop 8 slightly heaping tablespoons of batter into the oil. Fry the fritters about 4 to 4½ minutes, until golden brown. Use tongs or a slotted spoon to transfer the fritters from the hot oil to a baking sheet lined with paper towels. Allow the temperature of the oil to return to 350 degrees Fahrenheit before frying the second batch of 8 fritters. Keep the fritters warm in the preheated oven while assembling the salads.

FINISH AND ASSEMBLE THE SALAD

Divide and arrange the grapefruit and orange slices (alternately) in a circle near and around the outside edge of 4 room-temperature 12-inch plates. Vigorously whisk the citrus vinaigrette. Sprinkle the sliced citrus fruit on each plate with 1 tablespoon of vinaigrette. Place the curly endive pieces in a 7-quart stainless steel bowl. Vigorously whisk the remaining citrus vinaigrette, add it to the curly endive, and toss until the greens are coated with the vinaigrette. Divide and arrange an equal amount of curly endive in a mound inside the ring of sliced citrus fruit. Sprinkle 2 to 3 tablespoons of the port-soaked currants and raisins over the greens and sliced citrus fruit. Arrange 6 Belgian endive leaves in a starburst fashion in the center of each mound of curly endive. Place 4 warm mini fritters inside the starburst and serve immediately.

§

Mushroom-and-Onion-Stuffed Beef Tenderloin
Steak Variation

2 teaspoons extra-virgin olive oil
1 cup thinly sliced red onions
salt and freshly ground black pepper to taste
1/4 cup sauvignon blanc
1/4 pound shiitake mushrooms, stemmed and
   thinly sliced

1/2 teaspoon chopped fresh thyme
4 4-ounce beef tenderloin steaks, about
   1 inch thick

Heat 1 teaspoon of olive oil in a medium nonstick sauté pan over medium-high heat. When the oil is hot, add the onions. Season with salt and pepper, and cook, stirring frequently, for 10 minutes, until the onions are well browned. Add the sauvignon blanc and cook for 30 seconds. Add the shiitake mushrooms and chopped thyme, and cook for 6 minutes, stirring frequently. Transfer the mixture to a pie tin and place, uncovered, in the refrigerator to cool.

While the mixture is cooling, prepare the steaks for stuffing. Use a thin-bladed sharp knife to make a horizontal incision 1 inch wide and 1½ inches deep in the side of each steak. Use an index finger (wearing a food handler's glove makes sense for this task) to enlarge the pocket without actually poking through the sides of the steak. Stuff an equal amount (about 1 heaping tablespoon) of the chilled mushroom and onion mixture into each steak pocket. Season both sides of each steak with salt and pepper.

Heat the remaining 1 teaspoon of olive oil in a medium nonstick sauté pan over medium-high heat. When the oil is hot, add the steaks and cook for 2½ minutes on each side for rare to medium-rare, 3 minutes on each side for medium-rare to medium, 4 minutes on each side for a solid medium, and if so inclined, about 5 minutes on each side for well done. Transfer 1 hot steak directly from the pan to each salad or cool to room temperature and serve. (The cooled steaks can be refrigerated and served cold within 24 hours.)

🦎

Shad Roe Baked with Grain Mustard Variation

2 pairs shad roe

2 cups water

1 cup sauvignon blanc

¼ cup lemon juice

1 tablespoon kosher salt

2 tablespoons mayonnaise

2 tablespoons grain mustard

Preheat the oven to 425 degrees Fahrenheit.

Handling them carefully, rinse each pair of shad roe under cold running water. Using your hands, gently separate each pair and remove and discard the connective tissue.

Heat the water, wine, lemon juice, and kosher salt to a simmer in a large nonstick sauté pan over medium-high heat. Add the roe to the simmering water and cook for 3 minutes before using a spatula to turn the roe. Simmer for 3 more minutes. Transfer the partially cooked roe to a nonstick baking sheet.

In a small bowl, whisk together the mayonnaise and grain mustard until combined. Coat the top of each piece of roe with 1 tablespoon of the mixture, spreading to cover the entire top surface. Place the baking sheet on the center rack of the preheated oven and bake the roe for 9 minutes, until the coating is golden brown. Place a piece of roe on each salad and serve immediately.

The Chef's Touch

THIS SCINTILLATING salad draws its inspiration from a dinner salad we served at The Trellis. It had grapefruit sections dressed with a port wine vinaigrette and was served with blue cheese fritters. For this book's main course rendition, I decided that Dry Jack cheese would be better suited for the fritters, especially since these fritters were a focal point, not just an accent.

The Citrus Vinaigrette recipe yields ¾ cup. The vinaigrette may be kept at room temperature for 2 to 3 hours before using or refrigerated in a covered,

The Chef's Touch

noncorrosive container for 2 to 3 days. If refrigerated, return the vinaigrette to room temperature and whisk vigorously before using.

A true American classic, Dry Jack cheese is produced by aging Monterey Jack cheese. It has been a favorite of mine ever since I visited the Vella Cheese factory in downtown Sonoma, California, in 1989. My first taste of this sweet and nutty cheese was at lunch at a Sonoma County winery. After I learned that its source was just down the road, I made a beeline to the factory following the luncheon. Marketed under the Bear Flag label, the cheese can be purchased from specialty markets or directly from the folks that put this cheese on the map and on my table (see Sources, page 225).

Grapefruit is an odd citrus fruit. Growing in clusters like grapes despite its comparatively ungainly size, the grapefruit yields fruit that is sweeter than the lemon or lime but more assertively tart than the orange. The pink grapefruit adds a sparkle of color and a vibrancy of flavor to our unique salad. As with other citrus fruit, choose grapefruit that seem the heaviest for their size (they will be juicier).

I recommend using a sharp serrated knife to peel the grapefruit and oranges. Be certain to cut away both the colored skin as well as the white membrane under the skin. Called the pith, the white membrane is not only unsightly but also very bitter.

I prefer the smaller fritters for the sake of presentation, but you can make larger fritters based on your own tastes. (Count on a little extra frying time for larger fritters.) Try experimenting with other cheeses such as Gruyère or your favorite cheddar. (The amount of cheese used in the recipe should remain the same.)

Good-quality oil is critical for delicious and greaseless fried foods. Make certain the oil used is fresh; a container of oil once opened (especially if stored in a warm location) can become rancid. Whether for frying, sautéing, or salad making, for best results check the flavor of a previously opened container of oil before using.

One medium head of curly endive, about ¾ pound as purchased, should yield ½ pound of prepared greens. Two medium-size heads of Belgian

(continued on next page)

endive, about ¹⁄₂ pound, should yield 24 leaves. For crisp greens, spin-dry the washed curly endive pieces in a salad spinner. Gently wash and then pat dry the Belgian endive with paper towels; avoid bruising because this endive discolors easily.

My first experience cooking shad roe was exciting, if not dangerous. I was unaware of the explosive nature of these delicate egg sacks, and as I peered at an order cooking under a very hot open broiler, a loud cracking noise, followed by a spurt of steaming hot juices, startled me, although fortunately I was not scorched. Our method of preparing shad roe delivers a delicious and tranquil experience.

Suggesting a wine to accompany this salad was not as great a challenge as I had originally thought. As luck would have it, we introduced a new wine, the Ferrari-Carano Siena, at The Trellis the week before this salad recipe was tested at Ganache Hill. Upon first tasting this Sonoma, California, blend of Sangiovese, cabernet sauvignon, and merlot, I was struck by the remarkable flavor of fruit. Enhancing that was a perfect balance of acidity, just the sort of wine needed to work with the exhilarating flavors of this salad.

Equipment

Take a minute to notice the method to the madness in the Equipment section in each recipe. Each lists the tools needed in the order of their use in the recipe (for example, if the first ingredient in the recipe calls for ½ cup of walnuts, then the Equipment section will start off by listing measuring cups; or if the first ingredient in the recipe calls for six plum tomatoes, washed and cored, then the Equipment section will list a paring knife as the first piece of equipment). The section then continues by listing the tools needed for completing the recipes. Also, the item is listed only once in a recipe. (Measuring cups are not given more than once in the Equipment section, although they may be used several times in the course of preparing various ingredients throughout the recipes.)

Although I subscribe to the kitchen maxim of using the right tool for the job (an 8- to 10-inch cook's knife for slicing onions, for instance, rather than, say, a paring knife), I also believe in improvising when necessary. For example, a bowl and a saucepan make a fine double boiler. Having said that, here are a few pieces of equipment that I consider irreplaceable in the cook's cupboard.

FOOD PROCESSOR

Whether a recipe calls for pureeing scallions until smooth for use in a pasta dough (see Scallion Fettuccine, page 48), finely chopping pumpkin seeds for a smooth dressing (see Toasted Pumpkin Seed Dressing, page 154), or blending a dressing to form an emulsion (see Sherry Wine Dressing, page 43), a food processor will not only save the cook time but also will garner optimum results. The only downside is the cleaning, which should be done with care because the metal blade is so sharp that even some professional chefs (a well-known French chef from Philadelphia comes to mind) have lost digits when being careless in handling the food processor.

GRILL

Several of the meat, fish, or poultry options in *Salad Days* suggest grilling as the method of cooking these foods (in most cases an alternate means of cooking is also described). Some folks grill only during the summer months, but lots of others grill no matter the time of year or the weather conditions. At Ganache Hill I have an indoor grill that is essentially an insert that fits snugly into the fireplace. Manufactured by the Robert H. Peterson Company and marketed under the Fire Magic brand name, this grill is an economical way to enjoy grilled foods year-round (as long as your fireplace drafts properly).

With alfresco grilling (which I prefer, especially with an icy bottle of Budweiser in hand), I have cooked with a Weber Performer Grill for several years. Outfitted with a gas ignition system to light the fuel, this grill is practically trouble-free. A hibachi offers good results both indoors (put it in your fireplace) or outdoors (even a small apartment balcony will accommodate a hibachi). The only downside is that the small size of the cooking grate may limit your production.

JAPANESE TURNING VEGETABLE SLICER

I first learned about this piece of equipment while dining at The Mansion on Turtle Creek in Dallas, Texas. Chef Dean Fearing served a salad adorned with delicate ribbons of raw beets. After I marveled at how he transformed a rotund root into long slender ribbons, Chef Dean brought me back to the kitchen to proudly demonstrate an odd plastic gadget that effortlessly transmuted beets into seemingly endless strands. I was smitten.

I confess we went through a stage at The Trellis where we tried to cut almost every vegetable in our kitchen on the Japanese turning vegetable slicer. Easy and fun to operate, the turning slicer works best on solid and seedless vegetables such as carrots, turnips, potatoes, and the aforementioned beets. Turning slicers are available for less than $100 in Asian hardware stores or well-stocked cookware stores. If you are in the "trade," buy your turning slicer from the J. B. Prince Company (see Sources, page 225).

NONCORROSIVE CONTAINERS

When preparing and storing an acidic food such as a vinaigrette, always utilize noncorrosive equipment. Lengthy contact between a naturally acidic product like vinegar and a corrosive material such as aluminum will create an undesirable chemical reaction that may not only alter the flavor of the food but also make it less than healthful to ingest. In the Equipment section of each main course salad, I recommend stainless steel bowls over glass or plastic. I especially appreciate stainless steel when I drop a bowl on the ceramic tiles in my kitchen, and it dents rather than shatters.

NONSTICK PANS

My first job in the "business" was washing pots on weekends in a high-volume banquet hall in Woonsocket, Rhode Island, called the Bocce Club. I was fifteen years old. I must admit that my eagerness to "move up" and work in the pantry preparing salad was not driven solely by my nascent culinary pretensions. Rather, I was inspired by the frequent nightmares about the ceiling-high stacks of humongous roasting pans we used for chickens, and the oil barrel–sized pots that heated ever-thickening tomato sauce for pasta shells. Those memories played no small part in prompting me to stock our pot racks at The Trellis with quality nonstick cooking pans. Whether you cook at home or in a busy restaurant, nonstick cooking pans are not only easy to clean, but they allow the cook to sauté or pan-sear foods with a minimum amount of butter or oil, or even without fat.

RUBBER SPATULA

Don't leave anything behind—use a rubber spatula. To efficiently remove all the dressing, vinaigrette, salad, or whatever else, a rubber spatula is the right piece of equipment to scrape away every delicious ounce. I recommend a stiff, heavy-duty rubber spatula for mixing such items as the Roasted Root Vegetable Slaw (see page 177) or the Garbanzo Bean and Tomato Relish (see page 79). Heat-resistant rubber spatulas are now available and are perfect to use for sautéing, especially if you are cooking in a nonstick pan, since they won't mar the nonstick cooking surface.

SALAD SPINNER

The most effective way to rid salad greens of sand and dirt is to wash the greens gently in a sinkful of cool water, then remove the greens from the water (before draining the sink) and spin them dry in a salad spinner. Besides eliminating the grit, this also refreshes the greens and promotes crispness. If you have room, you may refrigerate the greens in the salad spinner until needed. The "Greens Machine" at The Trellis (a whopper of an electric-powered spinner with a removable 20-gallon capacity plastic insert) is such an integral piece of equipment in our pantry that both our longtime pantry supervisors, Clementine Darden (seventeen years of service) and Gisele Hicks (sixteen years of service), have said that without it they would consider early retirement! Truth is, I value Clem and Gisele so much that we keep extra parts for the Greens Machine on hand. If you don't have a salad spinner, shake the washed greens in a colander to remove excess moisture (residual water on the greens will dilute the flavor of the salad), then gently pat dry with paper towels. Refrigerate the washed and dried greens for 1 to 2 hours, until crisp.

SMOKER

Although smoking tobacco products has never been permitted in The Trellis kitchen, we have been smoking a variety of foods for years. We always have at least one or two smoked items on the menu, so we use a large professional-size smoker with precise temperature controls. For small-volume smoking, a number of economical and easy-to-use home smokers are available. The most basic is a stovetop smoker, which is available in cookware or hardware stores, or you can improvise with a 3- to 4-inch-deep pan, with a rack and a cover. Another popular home smoker is the "Little Chief," a brand we used at Ganache Hill to test the recipes in *Salad Days*. Larger than the stovetop-type smokers (it has a 20-pound capacity), the Little Chief has an electric element that creates the heat required to get the wood chips smoking. Whatever type of smoker you use, make sure that the smoking is done in a well-ventilated area, and if using a stovetop smoker, be certain to use your exhaust fan.

Practical Techniques and Useful Information

ॐ

PEELING AND SEEDING A TOMATO

Given that a medium-size tomato weighs a bit more than 6 ounces, I would venture that I have peeled and seeded 2 to 3 tons of tomatoes since graduating from The Culinary Institute of America in 1965. I'm not bragging, but I also am not certain all that peeling was necessary (it's primarily a matter of aesthetics). Seeding is another story. From both a textural and flavor standpoint, seeded tomatoes are far superior, with perhaps one exception—on sandwiches.

So after sharing my never-before-revealed feelings about this subject, let me get on with the tomato:

Core the stem end of a tomato with the tip of a sharp paring knife. On the opposite end of the tomato, use the tip of the same knife to score a ½- to ¾-inch **X** by cutting through the skin but not into the flesh. Immerse the tomato in boiling water for 30 to 60 seconds (the riper the tomato, the less time necessary; larger, underripe tomatoes will take more time) until the skin of the tomato begins to wrinkle and the skin at the scored **X** mark starts peeling away from the flesh of the tomato. Use a slotted kitchen spoon to remove the tomato from the boiling water, then immediately submerge the tomato in ice water. When the tomato is cold, 3 to 4 minutes, remove from the water and peel off the skin. In most cases the skin will slip off easily; however, if the tomato is resistant, use a paring knife to peel the skin away. If it is difficult even with a paring knife, that means the tomato did not spend enough time in the boiling water.

To seed a tomato, cut the peeled (or unpeeled and cored) tomato in half horizontally. Gently squeeze each half under cool running water, allowing the water to flush away the seeds. Peeled (or unpeeled) and seeded tomatoes may be stored in a covered, noncorrosive container in the refrigerator for 2 to 3 days.

SMOKING

One of the oldest methods of flavoring foods, smoking enjoys a significant popularity these days. Conceptualized as a means of preserving meats and fish, smoking along with drying and salting allowed the ancient cooks to stockpile foods for consumption during periods when hunting and fishing were not practical. At The Trellis we don't have to be concerned about the travails of stalking game, getting seasick, or camping in the wilds, thanks to the purveyors, farmers, watermen, and foragers who provide us with an eclectic mix of food all through the year. So flavor, not preserving, is our motivation to smoke a variety of food items.

The traditional technique for smoking most foods involves curing the item to be smoked in a brine for several hours or even for several days. A typical brine is composed of water, common salt (sodium chloride), and saltpeter (sodium nitrate). The primary function of a brine when used with animal protein is to stabilize the proteins and render them less susceptible to bacteria and spoilage. Additionally, the brine allows the flesh to more readily absorb the flavors of the smoke. Likewise, we cure most foods to be smoked at The Trellis, albeit for very short periods of time (minutes versus hours or more) because we are going for flavor only, not preservation. And for the sake of flavor we can introduce herbs, molasses, honey, vinegars, and even fruit juices into the brine to enhance the flavor of the smoked food.

Smoking is an economical means of creating excitement and diversity—in meat, fish, poultry, and vegetables—with enhanced flavors and unique textures.

SEASONING

Not so much a technique as a passion, seasoning enhances food by highlighting, complementing, and intensifying specific taste components. As elemental as adding salt and pepper to a particular food may seem, it can make the difference between a food's being good or tasting delicious. Seasoning, whether with salt and pepper or with herbs, spices, or other flavorings, can be done before cooking, during cooking, after cooking, or all of the above. Taste foods whenever possible during the entire cooking process to determine if the flavor development of the food needs to be enhanced, and then do so—but, for the most part, with a light hand. Remember that you can always boost flavor, but if food is overseasoned, it is difficult, if not impossible, to correct.

ROASTING AND SEEDING CHILES AND
BELL PEPPERS (CAPSICUMS)

The seemingly worldwide interest in Mediterranean cuisine has not only included indigenous ingredients and recipes but has also introduced techniques into the mainstream. The roasting and seeding of peppers is a case in point. Just a few years ago, if roasted peppers were needed in a recipe, the cook probably opened a can of pimentos (the fruit of a specific variety of capsicums—there are hundreds—but different from the bell pepper). Today, even novice cooks seem inclined to roast peppers rather than reach for the can.

Roasting mellows the heat in chiles and enhances the sweetness in bell peppers; it also creates a different textural mouth feel, making either pepper more succulent.

Both chiles and bell peppers can be roasted over a charcoal or wood fire, under a hot oven broiler, over a gas flame, or directly on an electric range element. Whatever method of heat is utilized, turn the chiles or peppers frequently while roasting in order to uniformly char and blister the skin. After roasting, remove the skin by rinsing the chiles or peppers one at a time under cold running water until the charred skin is removed. Next, pull the stem loose, then cut the chiles or peppers in half lengthwise and rinse each half under cold running water to remove the seeds. Remember to wash your hands immediately after handling chiles or, better yet, wear plastic food handler's gloves. The seeded chiles or peppers may be stored in a covered, noncorrosive container in the refrigerator for several days.

OVEN-ROASTING VEGETABLES

If you are passionate about big flavors, learning this technique will bring much joy to your table. Oven-roasting vegetables dissipates moisture and concentrates sugar. I first learned about oven-roasted vegetables in Italy several years ago (see page 41). Although that instructional experience was limited to tomatoes, experimentation with other vegetables at The Trellis finds us utilizing this method for flavor enhancement on an interesting mix of vegetables and even fruit (check out *Desserts to Die For* and my recipe for Oven-Roasted Peaches with Very Berry Yogurt). Oven-roasting is a simple technique with two important variables: length and heat.

Tomatoes must be roasted at low temperature (225 degrees Fahrenheit) for several hours, while most other vegetables such as carrots need to be roasted at a higher temperature (375 degrees Fahrenheit) for significantly less time. I learned this lesson well when I tried slow-roasting carrots while vacationing in Aspen a few years ago, with less than delicious results. I was preparing a dinner party for George Mahaffey, the executive chef of the Restaurant at Little Nell in Aspen, and I was also trying to save time so my wife, Connie, and I would not miss our daily hike. I put a baking sheet full of carrots in the same oven with a baking sheet of plum tomatoes, set the oven at 225 degrees Fahrenheit, went for a hike, and returned a few hours later to deliciously moist, succulent tomatoes but gnarly, tasteless carrots. I have also found that some vegetables benefit from being drizzled with oil, especially extra-virgin olive oil, before being roasted.

FASHIONING LEMON TWISTS

I learned how to fashion a lemon twist in a class on mixology (the study of preparing mixed drinks) at The Culinary Institute of America in November of 1963. Our instructor, John M. Dodig, the school's maître d'hôtel, taught us the art of mixing cocktails using colored water rather than spirits, and including flourishes such as lemon twists. Mr. Dodig's mixology class was memorable for many reasons, the most poignant being the day a student burst through the door to announce that President Kennedy had just been shot in Dallas. I have never forgotten the sense of loss and even despair I felt at that moment. On a more positive bent, I will always remember how to prepare lemon twists.

For the sake of aesthetics, select lemons free of blemishes. If you plan to use the juice, select fruit that seems heavy for its size (they will yield more juice). If you prefer less acidic lemons, look for fine-textured rather than coarse-skinned fruit, and those with a deep yellow color rather than those with a greenish cast. Rinse the lemons with lukewarm water before using.

Lemon twists and lemon zest are not to be confused. The former is a 2- to 2½-inch-long strip of lemon peel about ¼ inch wide, including the bitter white pith between the colored skin and the juice-laden fruit. The latter is usually very fine julienned strips of the colored skin only, without any trace of the bitter white pith.

For the most attractive and professional-looking lemon strips, use a very sharp, thin-bladed stainless steel knife (avoid carbon steel since it will interact with the acid and discolor the white pith). For less attractive although arguably more precise strips, use a lemon stripper (also called a channel knife).

When using a sharp, thin-blade knife, first cut off about ½ inch from each end of the lemon. Grasp the lemon in one hand with one of the ends facing upward. Make a cut into the colored skin of the fruit from one cut end to the other, cutting only to the depth of the white pith (avoid cutting into the juicy flesh). Repeat this cut at ¼-inch parallel intervals until the fruit has been cut all the way around. Use the tip of the knife to remove the strips of lemon, one at a time, from the fruit. The strips may be kept refrigerated for a couple of days in a tightly sealed plastic or other noncorrosive container.

If using a lemon stripper, don't trim the ends off. Grasp the lemon the same way previously described and use the stripper to remove lengthwise strips of lemon by cutting into the fruit about ¼ to ½ inch from one end and pulling the stripper towards you and down the length of the fruit, stopping about ¼ of an inch or so from the opposite end. Continue until the desired number of strips have been removed.

Before using, the lemon strips are given a twist to release the volatile lemon oil.

Bibliography

Cost, Bruce. *Bruce Cost's Asian Ingredients.* New York: William Morrow and Company, 1988.

Desaulniers, Marcel. *The Trellis Cookbook.* New York: Fireside/Simon & Schuster, 1992.

Ettlinger, Steve. *The Kitchenware Book.* New York: Macmillan Publishing Company, 1992.

Famularo, Joe. *The Joy of Grilling.* New York: Barron's, 1988.

Fussell, Betty. *The Story of Corn.* New York: Alfred A. Knopf, 1992.

Greene, Bert. *Greene on Greens.* New York: Workman Publishing, 1984.

Hazelton, Nika. *The Unabridged Vegetable Cookbook.* New York: M. Evans and Company, 1976.

Herbst, Sharon Tyler. *The New Food Lover's Companion.* New York: Barron's, 1995.

Knight, John B. *Knight's Foodservice Dictionary.* New York: Van Nostrand Reinhold Company, 1987.

La Place, Viana. *Verdura: Vegetables Italian Style.* New York: William Morrow and Company, 1991.

London, Sheryl and Mel. *The Versatile Grain and the Elegant Bean.* New York: Simon & Schuster, 1992.

Miller, Mark. *The Great Chile Book.* Berkeley, Calif.: Ten Speed Press, 1991.

Ody, Penelope. *The Complete Medicinal Herbal.* New York: Dorling Kindersley, Inc., 1993.

Ortiz, Elizabeth Lambert. *The Encyclopedia of Herbs, Spices & Flavorings.* New York: Dorling Kindersley, 1992.

Stone, Sally and Martin. *The Essential Root Vegetable Cookbook.* New York: Clarkson Potter, 1991.

Walter, Eugene. *American Cooking: Southern Style.* New York: Time-Life Books, 1971.

Waters, Alice. *Chez Panisse Vegetables.* New York: HarperCollins, 1996.

Sources

Dry Jack Cheese
Vella Cheese Co.
P. O. Box 191
Sonoma, California 95476-0191
800-848-0505

Grits
Byrd Mill Company
P. O. Box 1638
Gloucester, Virginia 28061-1638
804-555-1212

Country Ham
S. Wallace Edwards & Sons
P. O. Box 25
Surry, Virginia 23883
800-222-4267

Japanese Turning Vegetable Slicer
J. B. Prince Company
29 West 38th Street
New York, New York 10018
212-302-8611; fax: 212-819-9147

Quality Flour
The White Lily Foods Company
P. O. Box 871
Knoxville, Tennessee 37901
423-546-5511; fax: 423-521-7725

Quinoa, Wheat Berries
Rice River Farms
P. O. Box 550
Spooner, Wisconsin 54801
800-262-6368

Index

𝕊